MW00988333

The Withway: calling us home

Paul Cudenec

For those whom I love still and yet must live without

winteroak.org.uk

Cover illustration: *The Hilly Path, Ville d'Avray*, by
Alfred Sisley (1879)

Copyright © 2022 Paul Cudenec. The author formally
retains copyright over this work but permits non-
commercial reproduction or distribution

ISBN: 978-2-9575768-2-1

"In an ideal state of society one might imagine the good New growing naturally out of the good Old, without the need for polemic and theory; this would be a society with a living tradition"

T.S. Eliot, 'Reflections on Vers Libre'

CONTENTS

PREFACE

It has become a commonplace observation over the last couple of years, amongst dissidents thrown together in an epoch-defining struggle for freedom, that the left-right divide has no more meaning.

Perhaps this has always been the case, given the evident absurdity of trying to squeeze the whole glorious complexity of political and philosophical thought into a one-size-fits-all linear model. But at least the labels "left" and "right" provided, until recently, a rough idea of somebody's position regarding certain key social issues.

Now, however, even that approximate guide does not work. On the so-called "left", people who theoretically oppose both big business and the state are suddenly enthusiastic admirers of a toxic combination of the two, with their commitment to "fundamental human rights" replaced overnight with the conviction that it is "selfish" for individuals to resist the arbitrary dictates of power.

On the so-called "right", those who have

claimed to be trying to preserve a certain familiar way of life, guarantee a certain sense of order, have stood back and applauded as the society they always claimed to protect is subjected to controlled demolition and long-vaunted democratic values are abolished in favour of the kind of ruthless martial law that was supposed to be impossible in their "free world".

The separation today, between those who support the system's narrative and those who challenge it, simply does not follow the left-right divide. Another way of seeing the current situation is in terms of people versus power, as *below* versus *above*. While this is true as a kind of shorthand, which I have myself often used, it does not provide us with the *whole* picture of what we are facing.

The Withway is an attempt to identify the deeper issues at stake and point at a different way of seeing the civilizational choices with which we are being collectively presented.

It is not, as will be readily apparent, a political manifesto or a detailed programme for action. It is, rather, an exploration of ideas which is intended to act as a preliminary signpost, a rough sketch of the way in which many of us know intuitively we ought to be heading.

The primary direction in which we urgently need to move is, of course, away from the technocratic tyranny currently being imposed on us by force. In order to do so, we need to embrace and express the values which separate us from the cold "scientific" authoritarianism of the dominant cult.

In the pages that follow, I frame this in terms of re-establishing connections – social, natural and metaphysical – which have been stolen from us over a long period of time.

The overall perspective is holistic; not just in terms of seeing the whole picture, but in knowing that seeing the whole picture is *important.*

Within that overall reality, we could focus on the many fundamental differences between the way of being and thinking encouraged by the dominant system and the alternative which I happen to here term the Withway.

We could compare *their* power with *our* empowerment; *their* desire for control with *our* need for freedom; *their* lust for quantity with *our* quest for quality; *their* emphasis on price and profit with *our* commitment to value and fair exchange; *their* life-hating fetish for artificiality with *our* love for nature within and without; *their* twisted addiction to lies with *our* gut feeling for truth; *their* shallow, fragmented and subjective outlook with *our* profound and all-embracing organic vision; the ugliness of *their* world with the beauty of the archetype we hold in *our* hearts.

There is much work to be done in expanding, illustrating and joining together these themes, and many others, in a philosophy both ancient and new which can challenge and replace the deadthink of this toxic and moribund system.

I will try to play my small part in the months and years ahead, but if we are to have any real effect we are going to have to be numerous, creative and determined.

What name might we give this effort, what flag might we fly under on this ideological journey? I am not sure we can credibly give a label to a great movement of thought which is, in part, against the kind of mentality which always insists on labelling things!

But one will emerge, in due course, as it always does, and our task will be to ensure that the content of our thinking is sufficiently grounded, solid and authentic to stop that eventual label from being polluted, corrupted and turned against our intentions.

For this, depth of thinking is required; depth grown from eternal truths, rather than cobbled together from cheap slogans and passing fads.

In the ruins of this civilization, we need to plant a mighty tree of authentic wisdom that will watch over the health, freedom and future of humankind for many centuries to come.

Paul Cudenec, January 2022

PART I: NATURAL WITHNESS

In July 2021, more than a year into the global Covid "crisis", philosopher Augustin Berque gave an open-air talk in southern France, which I was able to attend.

The retired university professor spoke, all too briefly, from the shade of a marquee erected in the garden of the birthplace of Camisard resistance fighter Abraham Mazel, surrounded by the sunlit verdant hills of the Cévennes National Park.

In these inspiring surrounds, Berque outlined his study of what in French he calls "*la mésologie*" (the term 'mesology' has not yet taken root in English), which he says is "a new kind of knowledge"[1] taking us beyond the historical stage of modernity.

The fundamental idea, Berque said in his talk, was about respecting local realities and thus respecting their inhabitants in a complete context: "respecting their link with a territory is to respect our common link with the earth".[2]

As he set out in print in 2017, the connections between a person and the milieu in which they live cannot be erased. "Each of the two terms taken by itself is only half of reality. What *la mésologie* examines is precisely the combination of these two terms, which together make the whole reality".[3]

Berque argues that any landscape consists not only of measurable objects that materially surround us, but also of the perception that we have of it, stressing that "the reality of a landscape is in what takes place between the environment and our brain".[4]

He adds: "The milieu depends on the being and, vice versa, the being depends on the milieu. Each term supposes the existence of the other and also creates the other".[5]

This deep connection to place also takes us beyond the merely individual to the social, because it is something always shared with others: "To be fully human, we need our two halves, the one which is our physical individual body and the other which is our medial body, in other words our milieu, which is necessarily collective".[6]

One of the principal inspirations for Berque's outlook is the Japanese philosopher Watsuji Tetsurô (1889-1960), whose thought he regards as amounting to "a revolution in the history of being".[7]

Berque says: "With his vision of social organicity and of the social body (*aidagara*), he discovered a field of reality which turns the modern conception of existence upside-down by placing it back in an earthly environment... For Watsuji, the question of milieux (*fûdo*) concerns what physically creates and weaves together human societies, on this Earth".[8]

Watsuji identified a perpetual interaction between living beings and their milieu, leading to a mutual "appropriateness" between the two, which he termed *fûdosei*, the *médiance* which is at the heart of Berque's *mésologie*.[9]

In English, we might decide to translate *fûdosei* as "withness": the withness of place and inhabitant which means that neither could be what they are without the other.

Our withness means that we are never separate from the world that surrounds us, mere observers or spectators, cocooned in our egos and looking out on something which we can never finally be sure is real.

Instead, we are irrevocably part of that world, our being and emotions inseparable from all that is flowing around us.

Watsuji writes: "The springtime wind is that which scatters the cherry blossom or that which caresses the waves. The summer heat likewise, is that which withers the full-blooming greenery or that makes the children play on the beach. Just as we discover ourselves in sorrow or joy in the midst of the wind that scatters the flowers, it is

3

ourselves that we hear, drained of all energy, in the blazing sun which beats down on the trees. This is to say that we discover ourselves within *fûdo*, ourselves as a social organism".[10]

By seeing ourselves in our withness, we understand ourselves and can thus freely shape ourselves and the place where we live, he says in his classic book, *Fûdo*.[11]

Factors such as the climate, the soil, rain, heat and cold all inform the way in which we decide to build our houses, the kind of clothes we make and wear, the tools we fashion and use, the food we grow and eat.

This real experience, over many generations, of what the poet and critic T.S. Eliot refers to as "a particular people in a particular place",[12] accumulates to create what we sometimes label "tradition", which Eliot insists is no political abstraction or fixed idea to which we must remain welded, but living culture rooted in experience and always open to change.

For most of humankind's history, this place-withness (shared by nomadic as well as sedentary peoples) formed the basis of our living, creating a bond which would have seemed too obvious to need pointing out.

As contemporary philosopher Tu Wei-ming notes: "A natural outcome of primal peoples' embeddedness in concrete locality is their intimate and detailed knowledge of their environment; indeed the demarcations between their human habitat and nature are muted".[13]

When we picture birds in a wood, bees in a bank of flowers or fish in a stream do we feel the need to draw a hard line between birds and forest, bees and flowers or fish and water? Or can we conceive of them as belonging to one and the same phenomenon, as simultaneously birds-with-trees and trees-with-birds, as bees-with-flowers and flowers-with-bees, as fish-with-water and water-with-fish?

And ourselves? Can we still remember ourselves as people-with-the-land, as the-land-with-people?[14] Can we rediscover our identity in that living organic entity?

* * *

Tradition is not solely, or even primarily, the maintenance of certain dogmatic beliefs; these beliefs have come to take their living form in the course of the formation of a tradition... We are always in danger, in clinging to an old tradition, or attempting to re-establish one, of confusing the vital and the unessential, the real and the sentimental. Our second danger is to associate tradition with the immovable; to think of it as something hostile to all change; to aim to return to some previous condition which we imagine as having been capable of preservation in perpetuity, instead of aiming to stimulate the life which produced that tradition in its time.

T.S. Eliot[15]

* * *

When we live in and with a place, we do so alongside others.

Withness always tells of a collective level to existence, as Watsuji stresses when he reproaches the German philosopher Martin Heidegger for going no further in his search for authenticity than the individual level.[16]

For Watsuji, the notion of a human being (*ningen*) also embraces society, in the form of a community or a combination of people. "This dual character of the human is its fundamental character. It follows that neither anthropology, which only deals with one of its aspects, the individual, nor sociology, which only deals with its other aspect, society, can see the essence of humanity. To really grasp the core of human-kind, we have to understand the real structure of human existence, which is at the same time individual (*ko*) and whole (*zen*)".[17]

He explains that in traditional Japanese society "human conscience was that of the group" and "human totality was perceived as a mysterious force".[18]

In Watsuji's terminology, therefore, the word

ningen means not just a plain human being, but the human being complete in his essential withness.

How might we translate his *ningen* into English? Are we perhaps talking about withmen and withwomen? These withfolk experience what Watsuji calls *ningen sonzai* – human life in its full withness. They are experiencing not just bare existence, as individuals cut off from their community and their surroundings, but a whole and authentic belonging to the world of which they are part.

One of the foremost theoretical descriptions of this natural human withlife comes from the Russian thinker Peter Kropotkin

He argues in his best-known work, *Mutual Aid: A Factor of Evolution*, that the tendency for co-operation and solidarity is "deeply interwoven with all the past evolution of the human race".[19]

Kropotkin develops this theory in his unfinished work *Ethics: Origin and Development*, where he complains that those followers of Charles Darwin who regard competition between individuals as the key to evolution, have forgotten that the English naturalist himself identified the instinct of "mutual sympathy" in social animals.[20]

Adds Kropotkin: "On the basis of new investigations in the field of history it is already possible to conceive the history of mankind as the evolution of an inherent tendency of man to organize his life on the basis of mutual aid, first within the tribe, then in the village community, and in the republics of the free cities..."[21]

In 1902, the same year that Kropotkin published *Mutual Aid*, another radical thinker was advancing a similar theory on the way that living beings have a natural tendency to act together in the collective interest.

The Austrian Otto Gross, who was only 25 years old at the time, wrote an essay about *Synergetik*, or social energy, the force which binds together large numbers of individuals of all species. This could be observed in a school of young fish: "The entire school moves uniformly like an organism, particularly in fight or flight".[22]

This natural solidarity, says Gross, is an innate "will to relate":[23] an urge to withness which does not need to be taught.

Human beings are not separate, isolated units with no connection to those around them, any more than they are mere appendages of the collective, bound always to submit to its control.

Withness is always a two-way process, a relationship and not a hierarchy. The individual thrives as a free and fulfilled human being when she or he has the support of a community. A community thrives when it is made up of free and fulfilled human beings.

The richness is in the symbiosis.

* * *

Edward Carpenter (1844-1929) was a philosopher, writer and poet who, in the face of the growth of dehumanised industrial society, held out for a way of living based on freedom and solidarity.

He urged the modern person to rediscover themself as "the free child of Nature"[24] which they still were deep down.

To be true to this inner nature, a man had to cherish "his organic relation with the whole body of his fellows"[25] because it was this which held a free and natural society together.

When that organic order-from-below was gone, the door was opened to the supposed need for a state to come in and impose order-from-above.

Carpenter writes: "If each man remained in organic adhesion to the general body of his fellows no serious dis-harmony could occur; but it is when this vital unity of the body politic becomes weak that it has to be preserved by artificial means, and thus it is that with the decay of the primitive and instinctive social life there springs up a form of government which is no longer the democratic expression of the life of the whole people; but a kind of outside authority and compulsion thrust upon them by a ruling class or caste".[26]

* * *

Homage to thee, O Breath of Life, to thy crashing;
Homage to thee, the thunder; homage to thee, the
lightning;
Homage to thee, O Breath of Life, when thou
pourest rain.

The Atharva Vida[27]

* * *

"Birth and death, food and fire, sleep and waking, the motions of the winds, the cycles of the stars, the budding and falling of the leaves, the ebbing and flowing of the tides – all these things have, for thousands of years, created an accumulated tradition of human feeling",[28] writes John Cowper Powys.

He says it is the poetry of the real and the living, "the whole turbid stream of Nature, in its wild oceanic *ensemble*"[29] that is the authentic source of our spiritual well-being.

Powys refers to Jean-Jacques Rousseau's view "that the meaning of culture is nothing less than to restore, by means of our imaginative reason, that secret harmony with Nature which beasts and birds and plants possess, but which our civilization has done so much to eradicate from human feeling".[30]

"Human sensations are Nature's self-expression. They are the earth's awareness of herself. They are like the blossoming of flowers – the only way in which the rooted life of the organism can realize itself and *be* itself".[31]

* * *

From Wakan Tanka there came a great unifying life force that flowered in and through all things – the flowers of the plains, blowing winds, rocks, trees, birds, animals – and was the same force that had been breathed into the first man. Thus all things were kindred and were brought together by the same Great Mystery.

Standing Bear[32]

* * *

The understanding of the withness of people and nature is deeply embedded in traditional wisdom across the world.

It will come as little surprise to a modern Western reader to learn that a Native North American sun dance ceremony might contain the phrase: "The sky is my Father and these mountains are my Mother".[33]

But what about the similar statement that:

"Heaven is my father and Earth is my mother, and even such a small creature as I finds an intimate place in their midst"?[34] These are the words of 11th century Neo-Confucian philosopher Zhang Zai in China.

One of the defining characteristics of traditional Chinese political philosophy, explains James D. Sellmann, is its commitment to "the significance of cosmic harmony and its belief that this harmony is based on a reciprocal relationship obtaining between human life and the environment".[35]

Mary Eveyln Tucker adds that a "profound sense of the interconnectedness of the human with one another and with nature" is central to Confucian thinking, nature being "indispensable for sustaining communal life".[36]

Japanese Confucian scholar Kaibara Ekken (1630-1713) sees this withness as a harmonious spirit: "While the Wise know of its existence, the Foolish do not, for their hearts are heavy with selfish desire. This harmonious Spirit exists not only in man, but also in the birds, the beasts, and the fishes, and even in plants. Beasts play, birds sing, and fishes jump; while plants flourish, bloom, and ripen. They know how to enjoy that Spirit: man oftentimes does not".[37]

For Ekken, our heavenly and physical natures are essentially one and the same: "The fecundity of nature and the well springs of the human heart are seen as two aspects of the all-embracing process of change and transformation in the universe".[38]

J.J. Clarke credits Chinese Taoism with giving a particularly central role to nature, thus creating "a distinctive picture of the intimate relationship between the human and the natural worlds". He points out that Eastern thinking is holistic in outlook, refusing to draw any absolute distinction between the human and the natural worlds, or between mind and matter, but "seeing all such elements as inextricably entwined within an organic whole".[39]

* * *

The way is broad, reaching left as well as right.
The myriad creatures depend on it for Life yet it
claims no authority.

It accomplishes its task yet lays claim to no merit.
It clothes and feeds the myriad creatures yet lays
no claim to being their master.

Lao-Tzu[40]

* * *

Russian-Swiss scientist Constantin von Monakow devoted his life work to showing how

13

human beings are closely bound up not just with one another but with animals, plants and non-organic bodies, into which we merge after death.

He writes: "There is an undeniable glory in the thought that an indelible temporal bond links us, not only with our ancestors and our descendants, but above all also with the whole rest of the organic world".[41]

Natural withness is the essential reality of our existence, a reality which was very clear to those who lived and died before the advent of the industrial era.

"Our forefathers of fifteen hundred years ago lived not what we call 'close to nature' but actually *involved* with nature", writes Brian Branston. "They were not creatures apart, different from the birds, plants or animals, but fitted into the natural cycle of synthesis and disintegration which any kind of civilization always modifies".[42]

Withness is a belonging-to, a being-part-of. The boundary between me and that to which I belong is not solid, because I know that my very existence is rooted in that belonging. I am an extension of that which spawned me, which surrounds me, nourishes me, enchants me and welcomes my physical remains when my days are over.

French radical Georges Lapierre writes about the relationship between individuals in what are today described as "primitive" societies. Each person has their own outlook or vantage point, their own subjectivity, but others are seen as fellow subjects rather than as animated objects, mere walk-on extras in the film of one individual's all-important life.

He explains that this same withness is extended to the world beyond human community. Mountains, animals or plants are not seen as objects to be investigated or exploited, but as "subjects entering into a subject-to-subject relationship with men and women", [43] he says.

"The non-human environment isn't one empty of thought, it has nothing to do with our idea of nature, when all which is other is regarded as an object; instead it is a world of spirits, visible or not; it's a world of subjects with which the human subject is led to maintain a delicate relationship, all the more delicate since these non-human subjects, like human subjects for that matter, can prove to be touchy and powerful. This is a universe inhabited by subjects bound by the universal law of reciprocity, of gifts and gifts-in-return, in a world based on the exchange of all with all". [44]

In the withworld, these fellow subjects are not to be spurned, despised and despoiled, but must be respected and listened to for the wisdom they can bring us. Standing Bear, raised in this way of thinking, recalls: "The old people told us to heed *wa maka skan*, which were the 'moving things of the earth'. This meant, of course, the animals that lived and moved about, and the stories they told us of *wa maka skan* increased our interest and delight.

"Knowledge was inherent in all things. The world was a library and its books were the stories, leaves, grass, brooks, and the birds and animals that shared, alike with us, the storms and blessings of earth".[45]

The traditional human belief system gives every object in nature its own spirit and power,[46] and all of nature – animals, plants, mountains, forests, streams, landscapes – is understood to be animated by living intelligences or "spirits", with which people could be in communication.[47]

This supposedly outmoded outlook is not some kind of random bundle of superstitions and "unscientific" misunderstandings, as contemporary thinking would have it, but a solid basis for a profound and holistic understanding of our world and our existence.

"They have studied nature, drawn their conclusions from it, and found it to be the embodiment of a profound metaphysical principle pertaining to all existence", writes James G. Gowan regarding the Australian aborigines. "They have seen in it a symbol of an underlying reality which needs to be understood as sacred if true wisdom is to be attained".[48]

Natural withness therefore not only describes an authentic human relationship with the wider world, but an authentic *grasping* of that world, and our relationship to it, within our collective thinking.

"The system of Nature is at the same time the system of our mind," wrote the German nature philosopher Friedrich Schelling.[49]

Minds that work in partnership with external reality, which is sometimes termed "nature", rather than in denial of it, form themselves in accord with that reality, extend and develop that reality *as human thought*.

Withness is also within us.

* * *

Over the course of many millennia, our belonging to nature and our understanding of that belonging shaped itself into stories, myths and religious beliefs.

"It is from the constant awareness of the living connection between man and the phenomenal world that the myths of our ancestors arise, that their gods are born",[50] as Branston puts it.

Robert Graves describes how ancient Europeans worshipped the Great Goddess, the Lady of the Wild Things: "Dances were seasonal and fitted into an annual pattern from which gradually emerges the single grand theme of poetry: the life, death and resurrection of the Spirit of the Year, the Goddess's son and lover".[51]

In my own 2017 book *The Green One*, I present, as a multi-faceted composite character, what Varner describes as the vegetation spirits and gods which "are the foundations for classic and contemporary religious thought".[52]

I suggest that this idea, projected onto mythological characters from somewhere deep within the collective human soul, amounts to the knowledge that we cannot be separated physically or psychologically from the nature of which we are part. The Green One, whether in the guise of god or goddess, fairy or mermaid, Khidr, Robin Hood or Jack in the Green, is "the memory of this connection, the appreciation of this human belonging and of the fact that it must remain the untouchable foundation of our being".[53]

Watsuji, in his book on withness, takes a similar view of the origins of at least some strands of religious thought. He writes that the Greek gods were "nothing other than the divinisation of *external nature* (such as Zeus and Poseidon) or of *internal nature* (such as Aphrodite and Apollo)" and that gods of esoteric cults, like Mithras and Osiris, "were also divinisations of the forces of nature".[54]

He writes of India that "numerous hymns

are addressed not to the 'gods' but to 'nature', for example to the sun rather than to a god of the sun, to the water which flows or which falls from the clouds rather than to a god of water".[55]

"All the forces of nature are deified by reason of their mysterious character. It is not just the most visible things, like the sun, moon, sky, storm, wind, fire, water, dawn and earth, but also the forest, the savana, animals..."[56]

Sir James George Frazer, in his seminal work *The Golden Bough*, judges that the spring and harvest customs of European peasantry deserve to rank as "primitive", because they have not transformed aspects of nature into gods and goddesses in the way that the ancient Greeks or Egyptians did.

He writes: "No special class of persons and no special places are set exclusively apart for their performance; they may be performed by any one, master or man, mistress or maid, boy or girl; they are practised, not in temples or churches, but in the woods and meadows, beside brooks, in barns, on harvest fields and cottage floors.

"The supernatural beings whose existence is taken for granted in them are spirits rather than deities: their functions are limited to certain well-defined departments of nature: their names are general, like the Barley-mother, the Old Woman, the Maiden, not proper names like Demeter, Persephone, Dionysus".[57]

Demeter and Persephone, on the other hand, are anthropomorphic representations of the corn: "As the seed brings forth the ripe ear, so the Corn Mother Demeter gave birth to the Corn Daughter Persephone".[58]

Frazer notes that ancient rituals aimed at helping the revival of plant life in spring arose from the reality that "the life of man is inextricably bound up with that of plants, and that if they were to perish he could not survive".[59]

The same is evidently true of nature more generally and something which I did not explore through the vegetation-orientated character of The Green One was the way in which the behaviour and characteristics of our fellow creatures form the basis of what we now think of as purely human thinking.

Frazer points to "a time before the invention of husbandry when animals were revered as divine in themselves".[60]

These animals were, as we have seen, re-garded not as soulless objects but as fellow subjects – "the sharp line of demarcation which we draw between mankind and the lower animals does not exist for the savage".[61]

There was thus a foundation of a subject-to-subject relationship between the ancient human being and the animals on whom his survival depended.

"Even in the act of killing them he testifies his respect for them, endeavours to excuse or even conceal his share in procuring their death, and promises that their remains will be honourably treated".[62]

Frazer describes, for instance, how an Australian aboriginal ceremony depicts the witchetty grub, used as food, "in the act of emerging from the chrysalis".[63]

He records of the aboriginal Ainu people of Japan: "The skulls of slain bears receive a place of honour in their huts, or are set up on sacred posts outside the huts, and are treated with much respect: libations of millet beer, and of *sake*, an intoxicating liquor, are offered to them; and they are addressed as 'divine preservers' (*akoshiratki kamui*) or 'precious divinities'".[64]

And he explains that when the human sense of withness regarding an animal goes further still, there is a taboo against harming the sacred beast: "No consideration will induce a Sumatran to catch or wound a tiger except in self-defence or immediately after a tiger has destroyed a friend or relation. When a European has set traps for tigers, the people of the neighbourhood have been known to go by night to the place and explain to the animals that the traps are not set by them nor with their consent... The population of Mandeling, a district on the west coast of Sumatra, is divided into clans, one of which claims to be descended from a tiger".[65]

Meanwhile, "various tribes of Madagascar believe themselves to be descended from crocodiles, and accordingly they view the scaly reptile as, to all intents and purposes, a man and a brother".[66]

* * *

As human cultures gradually turned their deified animals into mythological characters and anthropomorphic gods, the original inspiration became harder, but not impossible to identify.

Frazer, for instance, regards the fact that the Phrygian Attis was killed by a boar, along with the fact that his worshippers would not eat swine flesh, as strong indications that he was originally a pig deity.[67]

Turning to Egyptian mythology, he writes: "The annual sacrifice of a pig to Osiris, coupled with the alleged hostility of the animal to the god, tends to show, first, that originally the pig was a god, and, second, that he was Osiris. At a later age, when Osiris became anthropomorphic and his original relation to the pig had been forgotten, the animal was first distinguished from him, and afterwards adopted as an enemy to him by mythologists who could think of no reason for killing a beast in connexion with the worship of a god except that the beast was the god's enemy..."[68]

Regarding the reasons why religious Jews, like Muslims, do not eat pork, he says "we must conclude that, originally at least, the pig was revered rather than abhorred by the Israelites... And in general it may perhaps be said that all so-called unclean animals were originally sacred; the reason for not eating them was that they were divine".[69]

There is a parallel here with the taboo on eating horse-flesh in Britain, as described by Graves. "The horse, or pony, has been a sacred animal in Britain from prehistoric times, not merely since the Bronze Age introduction of the stronger Asiatic breed. The only human figure represented in what survives of British Old Stone Age art is a man wearing a horse-mask, carved in bone, found in the Derbyshire Pin-hole Cave; a remote ancestor of the hobby-horse mummers in the English 'Christmas Play'. The Saxons and Danes venerated the horse as much as did their Celtic predecessors".[70]

The goddess Demeter (along with what Graves calls "Cernidwen the Welsh Pig-Demeter, alias the Old White One")[71] is also seen by Frazer as an evolution of pig-worship: "The pig was sacred to her; in art she was portrayed carrying or accompanied by a pig; and the pig was regularly sacrificed in her mysteries".[72]

The complication here is that Demeter is

also the corn-goddess and that "in European folk-lore the pig is a common embodiment of the corn-spirit".[73]

Frazer notes that Dionysus, too, was a deity of vegetation "often conceived and represented in animal shape, especially in the form, or at least with the horns, of a bull".[74]

"However we may explain it, the fact remains that in peasant folk-lore the corn-spirit is very commonly conceived and represented in animal form",[75] writes Frazer. "Amongst the many animals whose forms the corn-spirit is supposed to take are the wolf, dog, hare, fox, cock, goose, quail, cat, goat, cow (ox, bull), pig, and horse".[76]

Ultimately, all these mythological characters represent nature, and the representation of natural withness in the human collective mind. Nature knows no fixed boundaries: all is interdependent and intertwined.

* * *

Other manifestations of animal-withness in human mythology include:

* *Egyptian goddess Isis*. "Cows were sacred to her, and she was regularly depicted with the horns of a cow on her head, or even as a woman with the head of a cow".[77]

* *Greek goddess Athena.* "The goat was at one time a sacred animal or embodiment of Athena, as may be inferred from the practice of representing the goddess clad in a goat-skin (*aegis*)".[78]

* *Theban god Ammon.* "The ram was Ammon himself. On the monuments, it is true, Ammon appears in semi-human form with the body of a man and the head of a ram. But this only shews that he was in the usual chrysalis state through which beast-gods regularly pass before they emerge as full-blown anthropomorphic gods. The ram, therefore, was killed, not as a sacrifice to Ammon, but as the god himself, whose identity with the beast is plainly shewn by the custom of clothing his image in the skin of a slain ram".[79]

* *Italian deity Faunus.* Identical to the Greek Pan, he was "the son of Picus, which is Latin for woodpecker".[80]

* *Armenian goddess Anaitas.* She was derived from the lion-goddess Anatha Baetyl, according to Graves.[81]

* *Biblical cherub.* Mentioned in the first chapter of Ezekiel, in the Old Testament, it is also clearly a beast of the calendar sort, says Graves. "It has four parts which represent the 'four New Years' of Jewish tradition: Lion for Spring, Eagle for Summer; Man for Autumn, the principal New Year; and Ox for Winter, the Judaean ploughing season".[82]

* *Delphi, famed for its oracle.* Graves specifies that this ancient Greek site was sacred to "Apollo the Dolphin-God or Porpoise-god".[83]

* * *

Indian mythology, in which gods often take on animal forms, goes further in its sense of an essential withness between humans and the other beings with which we share this world, as Watsuji describes: "Even if we are currently human beings, in the next world we will perhaps exist as cows and in the previous world we were perhaps snakes. Correlatively, beings who are currently cows or snakes were perhaps previously humans, or one day will manifest as such. Thus, even if these creatures differ greatly in term of appearance, they all emerge from one sole substance".[84]

* * *

In his introduction to Frazer's *The Golden Bough*, Robert Fraser suggests that the real subject matter of the work is not immediately obvious. "Frazer's work might seem to be a compendium of ritual and custom. In fact it is something very different: a book on the human mind and the connections habitually made by it".[85]

The research and analysis was a kind of mental anthropology,[86] the study of what people have thought in the past, an uncovering of the layers of thinking which constitute universal human attitudes "and their different ways of expressing themselves in a variety of places and periods".[87]

Given the fact that Frazer's work clearly shows the way human belief-systems have emerged from our belonging to, interactions with and observations of nature, we could say that *The Golden Bough* describes the way in which our primal natural withness has been codified and absorbed into the collective human mind.

Kropotkin, too, saw the way in which our thinking had evolved from our closeness with fellow creatures.

He writes in *Ethics*: "Our primitive ancestors lived *with the animals, in the midst of them*. And as soon as they began to bring some order into their observations of nature, and to transmit them to posterity, the animals and their life supplied them with the chief materials for their unwritten encyclopaedia of knowledge, as well as for their wisdom, which they expressed in proverbs and sayings. Animal psychology was the first psychology studied by man – it is still a favourite subject of talk at the camp fires; and animal life, closely interwoven with that of man, was the subject of the very first rudiments of art, inspiring the first engravers and sculptors, and entering into the composition of the most ancient and epical legends and cosmogonic myths".[88]

While the primitive human may have initially simply related "these exploits of animals in his tales, embellishing the acts of courage and self-sacrifice with his primitive poetry, and *mimicking* them in his religious rites, now improperly called dances",[89] a deeper process was at work.

Kropotkin argues that it is here that we see "the natural origin not only of the rudiments of ethics, but also of the higher ethical feelings".[90]

Human notions of good and bad have been "borrowed from nature", he says. "They are reflections in the mind of man of what he saw in animal life and in the course of his social life, and due to it those impressions were developed into *general* conceptions of right and wrong. And it should be noted that we do not mean here the personal judgments of exceptional individuals, but the judgment of the majority. They contain the fundamental principles of equity and mutual sympathy, which apply to all sentient beings".[91]

In declaring that "nature has thus to be recognized as the *first ethical teacher of man*",[92] Kropotkin is careful to explain that alongside the "ethical lessons" which our primitive ancestors gained from the observation of nature, there are our "inherited *ethical tendencies*".[93]

He writes: "The social instinct, innate in men as well as in all social animals – this is the origin of all ethical conceptions and all the subsequent development of morality".[94]

This understanding is, like all real understanding, an old one. It was set out in the third century BCE by the Chinese Confucian philosopher Mencius.

For him, all the cardinal virtues such as *ren* (human-heartedness), *yi* (righteousness), *li* (courteousness) and *zhi* (wisdom) were innate to us, as pure potentials. "This means that everyone possesses these virtues 'to begin with'. If an individual is able to carry these beginnings into full development, the individual can become a sage",[95] explains Joseph S. Wu.

"His empirical argument states that when we observe a little child about to fall into a well, we experience a feeling of distress or alarm, and our natural response is to make an effort immediately to rescue the child. From this example we can conclude that our natural feeling does not allow us to tolerate the suffering of others. Such a feeling is universally innate in all of us, and this is the 'beginning' of human-heartedness".[96]

As Kropotkin identifies, we do not have to decide whether the lessons we have drawn from nature come from ancestral observation *or* from innate belonging – both factors are in play here.

Gross, who regarded ethics as arising from "a primitive instinct inherent in the human species",[97] specifically endorsed Kropotkin's suggestion that it was a question of both genetics and "normative discipline".[98]

* * *

Our natural withness means that we have evolved not in competition with nature nor alongside nature, but *with* and *within* nature.

The English poet William Wordsworth was
...well pleased to recognize
In nature and the language of the sense
The anchor of my purest thoughts, the nurse,
The guide, the guardian of my heart, and soul
Of all my moral being[99]

Human thinking and ethics have grown, in a particularly human way, from the seed of our natural belonging.

Berque writes: "Morality cannot be reduced to nature but neither can it be separated from its foundations in nature".[100]

Watsuji, too, is very clear on this matter,

remarking that we end up regarding the particularities of nature within us as being merely particularities of human life.

But, he says, humans are not born as clean slates unmarked by their natural withness: "We therefore have to see that the particularities of nature are something engraved in the spiritual structure of the human being, who is in this nature".[101]

* * *

When nature is able to express itself fully and clearly through the human mind and hand, its original beauty shines through.

For 19th century art critic John Ruskin and the Pre-Raphaelite movement he inspired, there was a withness in medieval society which remained visible in its artistic achievements, such as the great Gothic cathedrals of Europe.

Gothic, in Ruskin's eyes, was a form of art that was natural, human and beautiful, an art which expressed a social world of "tranquil and gentle existence, sustained by the gifts, and gladdened by the splendour, of the earth".[102]

These three qualities – natural, human and beautiful – always go together in Ruskin and the Pre-Raphaelites' shared vision and are contrasted with a modern industrial world which is artificial, inhuman and ugly.

Alfred Noyes depicts Ruskin as the prophet

of the new religion, "the religion of beauty".[103] He taught the young artists that it was in nature that they would find the aesthetic inspiration that had infused the Gothic cathedrals with their forest-like interiors, urging them to "go to Nature... rejecting nothing, selecting nothing and scorning nothing".[104]

"It is simply fuller Nature we want",[105] declared William Holman Hunt and the Pre-Raphaelites honoured not only the artistic tradition of the Middle Ages but also its way of thinking.

Ananda Coomaraswamy explains that from the medieval perspective, the form, beauty, goodness and truth of a thing are seen as deeply connected, almost synonymous.[106]

Art, like nature, is the outpouring of universal light. The individual artist is just one natural channel through which this light passes and makes its beauty visible, on a canvas or in a sculpture as in a mountain or a forest.

* * *

An understanding of natural withness lies at the heart of the work of German artist and theorist Joseph Beuys.

"It is not the case that first the earth must exist so that plants can grow in it, but rather that they have evolved hand-in-hand," he says.

"All matter arose through organic processes".[107]

He cites the example of bone, which comes into being by means of a natural process which remains visible.

"You can see that it has arisen out of fluid form, and so has spiral movements and vortices in it everywhere, very like vortex or spiral symbols. So it's really a rigidified fluid form. And if the bone is examined in detail you can still read the fluid form in it".[108]

As an extension of his idea of organic form in the structure of everything, Beuys describes human freedom as being founded on underlying natural order or "laws".[109]

He highlights the idea of a social organism, "a living being that we cannot today perceive with our ordinary senses, without practice".[110]

There is furthermore, he suggests, an archetype behind this social organism, an idea of what human community *would* look like if we were living in a condition of full natural withness.

* * *

The pattern of the human mind, the human essence, is something that has developed within nature.

This innate structure, with an inborn and natural sense of good and bad, right and wrong, ugly and beautiful, provides the basis of human

33

culture.

Codified into myths and religious beliefs, expressed as art and architecture, or regarded as basic decency or common sense, it is the force that gives pleasing shape to our lives, guiding the way we relate to each other and to the world around us.

Emerging naturally *from* our withness, it also speaks to us *of* our withness, of our dependence on and responsibilities towards our fellow humans, our fellow creatures and nature herself.

This pattern is natural order within us. It is the source of the social cohesion for which so many lost modern souls have yearned and sought, often blindly. Eliot, for instance, writes of James Joyce's groundbreaking novel *Ulysses* that the Irish writer's great conception was to use myth as a method for bringing order to the contemporary world.[111]

"Throughout Eliot's work the idea of pattern or order becomes the informing principle – he finds it everywhere, in literary tradition, in ritual, in political myth and in English history", writes biographer Peter Ackroyd.[112]

Eliot also sees pattern in the speech of ordinary people, which he seeks to reflect in his work. He stresses the need for a 'common style' in poetry, a 'common language of the people', the attempt to reflect 'the changing language of common intercourse'. "Even his understanding of musical pattern and musical form, which in practice was for him a deeply instinctive activity, was discussed in terms of the musical pattern which is 'latent in common speech'".[113]

Eliot himself explains: "Of course, we do not want the poet merely to reproduce exactly the conversational idiom of himself, his family, his friends, and his particular district: but what he finds there is the material out of which he must make his poetry. He must, like the sculptor, be faithful to the medium in which he works; it is out of sounds that he has heard that he must make his melody and harmony".[114]

The pattern of natural order is *dharma*, *asha*, humanity's withness to the structure of life, the order-from-within that informs our knowledge that not only do we have no need of external authorities and structures to bring "order" to our communities but that such authorities serve merely to destroy the organic order which arises naturally among us and thus they bring only *disorder* and social shattering.[115]

As Eliot's close friend the anarchist Herbert Read wrote: "There is an order in Nature, and the order of Society should be a reflection of it".[116]

* * *

Johann Wolfgang von Goethe approached this same issue from the perspective of botany, notably with his *Versuch die Metamorphose der Pflanzen zu erklären* (Metamorphosis of Plants) in 1790.

He detected the presence of innate principles throughout nature which provided a sense of direction and purpose to individual organisms.

This is the innate cohesion and order which renders artificially-imposed authority not only unnecessary but disruptive of our natural withness.

* * *

The patterns of nature are also, since we are part of nature, patterns in the human mind. But because we are human beings, these patterns manifest themselves in ways particular to humankind, such as through our rich traditional mythology, as we have seen.

Varner considers enduring mythology to be comprised of a "universal memory", a collective human awareness which recognises and describes the "inter-relatedness of the organisms on the Earth with the Earth itself, and the Earth in relationship with the universe".[117]

The origins of this universal memory in the patterns of nature within us explain why, despite the enormous diversity of what German ethnologist Adolf Bastian called *Völkergedanken*, or specific cultures, we are united by our common elementary ideas, *Elementargedanken*.

This is the "essential similarity"[118] identified by Frazer and what Joseph Campbell terms "the fundamental unity of the spiritual history of mankind".[119]

There are no dividing lines between physical and psychic reality, between the world outside us and the world within. Our minds are an extension of the patterns of the cosmos.

Our stories and beliefs are not so much human constructions as human filterings and rearrangings of the organic shapes, cycles and forces from which we are ultimately inseparable.

For instance, Radmila Moacanin explains that a *mandala*, the Sanskrit word for circle, is the round form found in all elements of nature, and in the arts and dances of all people, throughout history. "It is also an image residing in the depths of the human psyche that spontaneously emerges and assumes many different forms".[120]

Graves suggests that our word "circle" originates from the "circ-circ" cry made by falcons, known for their circling. This natural pattern also took the form, in human minds, of the goddess Circe. He says her name means "she-falcon" and he also links her to the use of the magical circle in various rituals.[121]

Carl Jung, the founder of analytical psychology, devoted his life to studying the origins and significance of this ingrained pattern in the human mind and its manifestation in mythology and religion.

"Mind is not born as a *tabula rasa*", he writes. "Like the body, it has its pre-established individual definiteness; namely, forms of behaviour. They become manifest in the ever-recurring patterns of psychic functioning".[122]

He identifies universal archetypes within the human psyche which underlie our thought processes at the deepest level and which remain dormant as *"forms without content*, representing merely the possibility of a certain type of perception and action".[123]

As Moacanin puts it: "Archetypes are not inherited ideas; they are merely propensities in the human psyche that can express themselves in specific forms and meaning when activated".[124]

* * *

Behind the Jungian concept of archetypes lies the assumption that there is a collective unconscious which is the common heritage of all humanity and the universal source of all conscious life.

Writes Moacanin: "In the depth of the collective unconscious, there are no individual or

38

cultural differences, no separation. It is the realm of primordial unity, nonduality, and through it each person is connected with the rest of humanity".[125]

But the withness implied by these deeply-etched patterns goes further than our human and natural withness: they reveal our essential belonging to the universe as a whole.

This cosmic withness was embraced by the traditional wisdom which illuminated our existences for many thousands of years.

Silvia Federici describes it as a "magical view of the world which, despite the efforts of the Church, had continued to prevail on a popular level through the Middle Ages".

She explains: "At the basis of magic was an animistic conception of nature that did not admit to any separation between matter and spirit, and thus imagined the cosmos as a living organism, populated by occult forces, where every element was in 'sympathetic' relation with the rest".[126]

Lapierre likewise depicts an old way of thinking from which we might draw inspiration: a system of thought which posits "an intimate solidarity"[127] between the human individual, human society and the universe.

"The human being is at the centre of a communication network on a cosmic scale, at the centre of a network of universal correspondences. We find this hard to accept".[128]

This wider context is the bedrock of all traditional metaphysical understanding, even though this with-wisdom – or should we simply say "withdom"? – remained more visible and accessible in non-Western belief systems.

Sarvepalli Radhakrishnan, the important Indian philosopher who was president of his country between 1962 and 1967, explains: "If science teaches us anything, it is the organic nature of the universe. We are one with the world that has made us, one with every scene that is spread before our eyes. In a metaphor common to the Upanishads and Plato every unit of nature is a microcosm reflecting in itself the entire all-inclusive macrocosm...

"We are solid with the world and are deeply rooted in it. We are not merely spectators of the universe but constituent parts of it".[129]

Another Indian thinker, Sri Aurobindo, writes that "the self and the world are in an eternal close relation and there is a connection between them, not a gulf that has to be overleaped... This is the realisation which the ancient Vedantins spoke of as seeing all existences in the self and the self in all existences".[130]

Aurobindo says that our self is not the individual mental being usually identified as such, but that which is sourced from our deep withness and is "one with all existence and the inhabitant of all existences". He adds: "The self behind our mind, life and body is the same as the self behind the mind, life and body of all our fellow-beings".[131]

Chinese Confucian thought is also based on "anthropocosmic unity", notes Chenyang Li: "One way to describe this metaphysic is that Heaven and man are an inseparable single oneness".[132]

And the world of withness is never about a one-way relationship, but about what Alan Fox, summarising the ideas of Fazang (643-712), a philosopher from Samarkand in Central Asia, describes as "the interpenetration of phenomena with principle and with each other without obstruction".

He continues: "In some sense, this can be understood as the relation between a context and the elements which make up the context – the context depends on its elements just as the elements are meaningless outside of a context".[133]

Here is Berque's *médiance*, with which I began this section, interpreted on a metaphysical level. Our withness to all that surrounds us is centred not on the personal or the universal, nor even on both together, but on their interdependence and ultimate inseparability.

PART II: LOST IN FALSEHOOD

Come away, O human child!
To the waters and the wild
With a faery, hand in hand,
For the world's more full of weeping than you can
understand

W.B. Yeats[1]

As I write these words, humankind has never seemed further from a condition of natural withness.

In 2013, I warned that "the normal, healthy, interconnections of a society, the neural pathways that enable it to function as a whole, have been blocked by disease – the disease of modernity"[2] with the result that it is now "almost impossible to lead a truly meaningful life".[3]

Over the last two traumatic years, still more layers of separation have been added to this already-serious loss of authenticity.

The ideal of social withness has been directly

countered by a new cult of "social distancing", in which all direct unmediated contact with our fellow human beings is regarded as dangerously irresponsible.

Henceforth, in the twisted vision of the Great Reset publicised by Klaus Schwab of the World Economic Forum, all our interactions should take place within the digital framework constructed around us by a predatory ruling class.

We are ordered to distrust each other, to mask our faces and thus our emotions, to avoid talking, singing, hugging, kissing or even shaking hands.

Solidarity is out of bounds: those who do not conform to the *diktats* of authority are depicted as not only unworthy of empathy or support but as positive threats to the well-being of the credulous majority.

Any talk of freedom is interpreted as selfishness, any expression of individual opinion as anti-sociality, any critical thinking as conspiracy theory, any revelation of inconvenient truth as disinformation, any deviation from, or questioning of, official dogma as criminality.

Even our withness to our own bodies has come under unprecedented attack, our physical integrity denied in the same toxic pharmaceutical breath as the existence of our natural immune systems.

Transhumanism, once seen as a peripheral cult of semi-crazed life-hating fantasists, has now revealed itself to be the official religion of the worldwide global establishment: a dominant death-cult possessed of enormous financial wealth and thus power.

We are faced with the possibility of a nightmare future in which the very essence of humanity has been destroyed, in which every last one of us has been removed from our natural belonging to each other and to nature and reduced to the status of units of human capital in a digital economy, our life-energy harvested for the profit and pleasure of a clique of venal and sociopathic parasites.

How on earth did we get to this point?

* * *

The general name we could give to everything that assaults, undermines, pollutes and destroys our natural withness is "power".

Power is a form of separation. A human being who seeks power over another has ceased to regard that person as a fellow subject and treats them instead as an object. The denial of withness, of mutual sympathy, with fellow human beings breaks the natural bond which creates natural order.

By treating any fellow human being as less

than human, power-seekers abandon their own full human identity as withfolk. In considering themselves to be better than others, whom they see fit to use as objects for their own self-advancement, they are effectively removing themselves from the realm of right-living, from *dharma*, from the collective ethical sense that makes us fully human.

In attempting to increase their own status or level of comfort by walking on the backs of those they consider beneath them, they fall down to a condition beneath that of authentic humanity.

The same applies when such incomplete humans, half-humans lacking the withness essential to our shared humanity, refuse to see their innate withness to nature and instead regard fellow creatures or living eco-systems as objects, lower than them, from which they consider they are entitled to extract the material wealth with which they maintain and expand their power over other human beings.

* * *

There are many and diverse theories about how and when power-based relationships entered into human society – or, more specifically, how and when they crept beyond the purely personal (and thus ephemeral) to become a systematically embedded blockage to our natural withness.

Some maintain that it was in abandoning a nomadic way of life and taking up agriculture that our ancestors adopted a hierarchical social structure that would evolve into the modern state.

But James C. Scott, in his 2017 book *Against the Grain: A Deep History of the Earliest States*, takes a slightly different view.

He reminds us that the first evidence of cultivated plants and of sedentary communities appears roughly 12,000 years ago: "Until then – that is to say for ninety-five percent of the human experience on earth – we lived in small, mobile, dispersed, relatively egalitarian, hunting-and-gathering bands".[4]

He points to the fact that the first very small, stratified, tax-collecting walled states emerged in the Tigris and Euphrates Valley only around 3,100 BCE, in other words several millennia *after* the first crop domestications and sedentism.

Scott writes: "This massive lag is a problem for those theorists who would naturalize the state form and assume that once crops and sedentism, the technological and demographic requirements, respectively, for state formation were established, states/empires would immediately arise as the logical and most efficient units of political order".[5]

He concludes: "Clearly our ancestors did not

rush headlong into the Neolithic revolution or into the arms of the earliest states".[6]

So while the adoption of an agricultural lifestyle certainly *made possible* the emergence of states, ruling over and taxing settled populations, it did not automatically bring it about. Another agricultural world was demonstrably possible.

Scott raises the question as to what it was, then, that after thousands of years of agriculture, suddenly pushed free communities into power-based state structures.

Did people suddenly decide they would like to live under the control of a central authority which had the right to confiscate their produce, conscript them into its armies and so on? Or were they forced?

He muses: "If the formation of the earliest states were shown to be largely a coercive enterprise, the vision of the state, one dear to the heart of such social-contract theorists as Hobbes and Locke, as a magnet of civil peace, social order, and freedom from fear, drawing people in by its charisma, would have to be reexamined".[7]

If the first states used coercion to establish their rule, then they were criminal enterprises and the whole of our state-based civilization since then has been built on a foundation of crime. Violent crime, in fact, because force (both inflicted and threatened) has always been the mainstay of state control.

The motive for this crime is clear: populations under state control could be forced to produce surpluses which would enrich the ruling family or clique, enabling them to build up ever-greater material wealth with which to pay those who violently imposed their criminal control.

Scott draws out the reality of the state's essential criminality by exploring the role of early "barbarians", which is to say peoples who were not yet incorporated into states.

They initially flourished alongside the early states by plundering the surpluses produced at the behest of those states. State rulers often ended up paying them not to carry out these raids. Since the money used to pay them off came from the exploited population, people were effectively being taxed by their enemies.

As Scott says, this amounts to a protection racket, of the kind carried out by modern day criminal mafia, in which the threat of violence is used to extract money from the victim.

He writes: "Protection rackets that are routine and that persist are a longer-run strategy than one-time sacking and therefore depend on a reasonably stable political and military environment. In extracting a sustainable surplus from sedentary communities and fending off external attacks to protect its base, a stable protection racket like this is hard to distinguish from the archaic state itself".[8]

The early agrarian states and the barbarian entities were effectively "competing protection rackets",[9] he stresses.

Because states themselves draw up the rules by which their societies operate, their definitions of "legal" and "illegal" will never identify their own existence as being fundamentally criminal.

But the violent coercion on which state rule depends is a crime nonetheless, according to the innate human sense of right and wrong, the natural ethics which form the ordered pattern behind authentic human communities.

This ugly reality is illustrated by the way in which, from the very start, states regarded and treated human beings – not as subjects but as objects.

"A peasantry – assuming that it has enough to meet its basic needs – will not automatically produce a surplus that elites might appropriate, but must be compelled to produce it", writes Scott.

"Only through one form or another of unfree, coerced labor – corvée labor, forced delivery of grain or other products, debt bondage, serfdom, communal bondage and tribute, and various forms of slavery – was a surplus brought into being".[10]

He says evidence overwhelmingly confirms that bondage was a condition of the ancient state's survival: "States, we know, did not invent slavery and human bondage: they could be found in innumerable prestate societies. What states surely did invent, however, are large-scale societies based systematically on coerced, captive human labor".[11]

Unfree labour was needed to build city walls and roads, dig canals, to carry out mining, quarrying, logging, monumental construction and agriculture.

Violent coercion was the means by which men could be forced to work for the state, and archaeological evidence from ancient Mesopotamia indicates that slaves and prisoners of war were not treated well, many being depicted in neck fetters or being physically subdued.

Write Hans J. Nissen and Peter Heine: "On cylinder seals we meet frequent variants of a scene in which the ruler supervises his men as they beat shackled prisoners with clubs".[12]

The state saw itself as *owning* the people it ruled over (what greater crime could one imagine than the theft of one's own person?) and regarded its population as human livestock, says Scott, "as a form of wealth".[13]

Thus walls around cities, or great walls across China, were not so much intended to keep the barbarians out as to keep the human cattle inside the state corral: "One of the hallmarks of early statecraft in agrarian kingdoms was to hold the population in place and prevent any unauthorized movement. Physical mobility and dispersal are the bane of the tax man",[14] writes Scott.

"The state remained as focused on the number and productivity of its 'domesticated' subjects as a shepherd might husband his flock or a farmer tend his crops. The imperative of collecting people, settling them close to the core of power, holding them there, and having them produce a surplus in excess of their own needs animates much of early statecraft".[15]

The development of the state was a deliberate move by a band of organised criminals to "move beyond sheer plunder and to more rationally extract labor and foodstuffs from their subjects",[16] as Scott puts it.

Even in their earliest form, calculation and statistics were used by the robber-tyrants to reduce fellow human beings to numbers on a list, to mere objects to be exploited for profit and power.

Receipts, work orders and labour dues quickly made an appearance and "something like 'work points' were created showing credits and debits in work assignments".[17]

Early written records from Uruk show that, in state accounts, the age and sex categories used to list human labourers were exactly the same as those used to describe "'state-controlled herds of domestic animals", suggesting an equivalent social status, as Guillermo Algaze has commented.[18]

Similarly, women slaves of reproductive age were prized in large part as "breeders"[19] because of their contribution to the early state's manpower machine.

Our communal strength and sense of freedom, which might lead to rebellion, arise from our withness and so had to be destroyed by the tyrants running the early states.

Slaves were drawn from scattered locations and backgrounds, separated from their families and communities. They were thereby "socially demobilized or atomized and therefore easier to control", explains Scott. "Having, unlike local subjects, few if any local social ties, they were scarcely able to muster any collective opposition".[20]

* * *

"Every State constitutes an alliance of the rich against the poor, and of the ruling classes, i.e., the military, the lawyers, the rulers, and the clergy, against those governed",[21] writes Peter Kropotkin in *Ethics*.

We might go further and say that every state constitutes a crime committed by the rich against the poor, by the self-appointed ruling classes against the victims of their endless self-serving violence.

We see this same picture again and again throughout history. The Roman Empire, such an inspiration for Western Civilization as a whole, and not merely for fascism, was characterised by its central control, its "tension towards integration"[22] as Watsuji Tetsurô terms it.

Slavery, of course, went hand in hand with the accumulation of imperial wealth and power.

Scott writes: "Imperial Rome, a polity on a scale rivaled only by its easternmost contemporary, Han Dynasty China, turned much of the Mediterranean basin into a massive slave emporium. Every Roman military campaign was shadowed by slave merchants and ordinary soldiers who expected to become rich by selling or ransoming the captives they had taken personally.

"By one estimate, the Gallic Wars yielded nearly a million new slaves, while in Augustan Rome and Italy, slaves represented from one-quarter to one-third of the population. The ubiquity of slaves as a commodity was reflected in the fact that in the classical world a 'standardized' slave became a unit of measurement: in Athens at one point – the market fluctuated – a pair of working mules was worth three slaves".[23]

When European states embarked on building a more recent empire, slavery again played a key role. Adam Hochschild has observed that as late as 1800 roughly three-quarters of the world's population could be said to be living in bondage.[24]

If outright slavery subsequently became less prevalent, it was perhaps because it was no longer even necessary.

"When population becomes so dense that land can be controlled it becomes unnecessary to keep the lower classes in bondage; it is sufficient to deprive the working class of the right to be independent cultivators",[25] writes Ester Boserup.

Deprived of our withness to the land, we are deprived of our autonomy and so at the permanent mercy of the violent criminal class who stole everything from us.

* * *

.... Men have forgotten
All gods except Usury,
Lust and Power

T.S. Eliot[26]

* * *

The iniquitous role of the state is identified by the ground-breaking German sociologist Ferdinand Tönnies (1855-1936) in his best-known work, *Community and Society*.

He concludes that it amounts to "nothing but force"[27] and totally undermines the possibility of organic social cohesion in "a natural order in which every member does his part harmoniously in order to enjoy his share".[28]

Ordinary people are very aware that the state is their enemy, he says. "The state, to them, is an alien and unfriendly power; although seemingly authorized by them and embodying their own will, it is nevertheless opposed to all their needs and desires, protecting property which they do not possess, forcing them into military service for a country which offers them hearth and altar only in the form of a heated room on the upper floor ..."[29]

It is not by chance that Tönnies was also an outspoken critic of the commercial mentality that underlies modern society.

Commerce is about making money, gaining wealth and thus power, at the expense of other human beings. It breaks from the innate human ethics of withness and social solidarity and instead proposes a dog-eat-dog anti-morality, in which all sense of right and wrong is swept away by the pursuit of egotistical and material ends.

It was, as we have seen, this sociopathic craving for power over others which motivated the criminal gangs who first set themselves up as "authorities" and built all the apparatus of the state to justify and defend their historical theft from the commons.

Tönnies identifies a social decline from traditional organic community, *Gemeinschaft*, into the top-down artificiality of modern society, *Gesellschaft*.

He writes: "The merchants or capitalists (the owners of money which can be increased by double exchange) are the natural masters and rulers of the Gesellschaft. The Gesellschaft exists for their sake. It is their tool".[30]

The move to Gesellschaft "meant the victory of egoism, impudence, falsehood, and cunning, the ascendancy of greed for money, ambition and lust for pleasure".[31]

* * *

The commercial mindset places quantity above quality, price above value, glitter above substance.

It reduces human beings to units of production and consumption, to the means for its own enrichment.

It was this mindset that lay behind the Utilitarian movement in 18th and 19th century Britain, as Theodore Roszak sets out in *The Cult of Information*.

Although they claimed to follow scientific objectivity, Utilitarians such as Jeremy Bentham were in fact inspired by "a definite political ideology, a not-so-very-hidden agenda",[32] he writes.

Their "perfectly dismal vision of human nature and a grim obsession with cash values" led them to believe that the poor should be whipped to work. "This made them the allies of factory owners who had reduced the conditions of labor to an inhuman level. It would be no exaggeration to say that, with the lash of pure fact in their hands, the Benthamites helped produce the work force of the industrial revolution".[33]

* * *

Business presents itself as some kind of entity separate from the state, but needs the state to impose its exploitation on the population.
Business therefore needs to control the state and can never allow genuine democracy to come in the way of its needs.
Business is nothing other than theft, but because business controls the state, this theft is regarded as legitimate.

Organic Radicals website[34]

* * *

58

The "work ethic" embraced by slavemasters ancient and modern is one of the many symptoms of our loss of withness.

As creatures who belong to the Earth, to nature, we naturally evolved to flourish and feed ourselves from the fruit of the land, as does other every other living being within the planetary organism.

But a barrier has been erected. The resources which are our collective birthright no longer belong to us, but to a class of thieves who have claimed them for their own and have so much accumulated wealth and power that they can deploy unlimited violence to keep hold of their loot.

We are therefore obliged to work for these criminals, to give our labour for their still-greater enrichment, simply in order to have the right to live somewhere, to drink water, to clothe and feed ourselves and our families.

Although camouflaged by talk of salaries and contracts and trades and careers, as well as by the crumbs of minor luxuries that fall into our mouths from the tables of the wealthy overclass, the bondage is as real as that endured by the slave-labourers of ancient Mesopotamia.

* * *

In her book *Caliban and the Witch*, Silvia

Federici rejects the received wisdom that a "transition to capitalism" formed part of a kind of natural social evolution.

Instead, she says, it was a response by the European ruling class to a mighty wave of popular revolt in the Middle Ages which threatened their domination.

She writes: "Capitalism was the counter-revolution that destroyed the possibilities that had emerged from the anti-feudal struggle – possibilities which, if realized, might have spared us the immense destruction of lives and the natural environment that has marked the advance of capitalist relations worldwide. This much must be stressed, for the belief that capitalism 'evolved' from feudalism and represents a higher form of social life has not yet been dispelled".[35]

The Middle Ages, she explains, were a period of "relentless class struggle" in which "the medieval village was the theater of daily warfare".[36]

"Everywhere masses of people resisted the destruction of their former ways of existence, fighting against land privatization, the abolition of customary rights, the imposition of new taxes, wage-dependence, and the continuous presence of armies in their neighbourhoods, which was so hated that people rushed to close the gates of their towns to prevent soldiers from settling among them".[37]

So as to impose their system on the unwilling people, the power elite used "social enclosure",[38] Federici says. "In pursuit of social discipline, an attack was launched against all forms of collective sociality and sexuality including sports, games, dances, ale-wakes, festivals, and other group-rituals that had been a source of bonding and solidarity among workers".[39]

* * *

The fracturing of human withness, in all its aspects, can be seen as resulting from the psychological separation of the individual from the social and physical milieu, the forgetting of the bonds of mutual sympathy that tie us to each other and to the physical context of our lives.

The ruling gang of criminals not only cast aside empathy and solidarity in their quest for power, but also instil that same flaw in others and depend on that social fragmentation to prevent the huge majority from combining against their domination.

Chinese philosopher Mozi had already identified this danger in the fifth century BCE. "The social crisis of his times, according to Mozi, stems from selfishness, or what he calls partiality," outlines Lawrence F. Hundersmarck.

"When the ruler of one state thinks only of gaining advantage over the ruler of another state, or when one family seeks its own ends over all other families, the resulting narcissistic self-preoccupation generates a disease of partiality that destroys society".[40]

Recent consumer society, which has polluted even supposedly critical political currents with its me-first off-the-peg individualism, has dragged this narcissism to new depths.

Behind the tendency, we can see a deep ideological attachment to separation, a fanatical opposition to any idea of solidarity or holistic withness, which informs the dogma of modernity often labelled liberalism.

Complains Eliot: "These liberals are convinced that only by what is called unrestrained individualism will truth ever emerge. Ideas, views of life, they think, issue distinct from independent heads, and in consequence of their knocking violently against each other, the fittest survive, and truth rises triumphant. Anyone who dissents from this view must either be a medievalist, wishful only to set back the clock, or else a fascist, and probably both".[41]

But, at the same time, the contemporary system also denies *true* individuality in its demand for total conformity and obedience. The cogs in their machine are not supposed to think and act autonomously.

Kropotkin, that great exponent of collective mutual aid, notes with concern the steady growth of "the subjection of the individual – to the war machinery of the State, the system of education, the mental discipline required for the support of the existing institutions, and so on" and warns of "the presumption of a still greater absorption of the individual by society".[42]

He concludes that "the want of development of the personality (leading to herd-psychology) and the lack of individual creative power and initiative are certainly one of the chief defects of our time".[43]

On this road apart on which we have all been forced to travel, the natural order of our world has been left far behind.

Authentic individual development gives each of us the confidence and capacity to become all that we could have been and to thus to enrich the collective life of the community of which we are part.

Selfish individualism is a stunted growth, a twig of life that never blossoms and brings no beauty to the bare, diseased tree of a humanity ripped out of the soil of natural withness.

* * *

John Cowper Powys writes in *The Meaning of Culture*, first published in 1929, that if you look and listen for a moment in the modern world you are sure to find something "that is so repulsive to you, so poisonous to your nature, so contrary to all your ideas of what beauty is, and what truth is, and what noble simplicity is, that it will scarcely bear thinking on".[44]

* * *

Psychoanalyst Otto Gross explores the way in which individuals are mentally crushed by artificial contemporary society.

Fearful of being rejected and unloved by those around us, we stifle our inborn potential so as to fit in.

Gross writes: "The fear of loneliness, the drive for contact, forces the child to adapt: the suggestions from foreign will that one calls education are incorporated into one's own will. And so the majority consist almost solely of foreign will that they have incorporated, of the foreign type to which they have adapted, of the foreign being that appears to them completely to be their own personality...

"They have spared themselves an inner divisiveness; they have adapted to things as they are. They are the majority".[45]

* * *

Our essential human identity, as withfolk, arises from our symbiotic relationship with our own milieu, community and culture.

Therefore, paradoxically, the more we embrace the particularities which constitute our personal withness, the more we become a general example of humanity fulfilling its true innate potential.

As Eliot writes of W.B. Yeats: "In becoming more Irish, not in subject-matter, but in expression, he became at the same time universal".[46]

* * *

Money is a tool. For dominated and exploited individuals, it is the tool by which they can regain the basic right to food, shelter and warmth stolen from them by the ruling class along with their social and natural withness.

For the dominating and exploiting criminal class, money is the tool by which they can make individuals participate in, and become totally dependent upon, the system they have created in their own interests.

Little matter if once-free people had devised their own systems of exchange and mutual gifts which worked perfectly for them. Once money-power takes control, it will demand tributes and taxes be paid to it in the currency it has invented and controls. This money can only be obtained by participation in its own structures of exploitation.

Money is the means by which the ruling criminals can solidify the power they grabbed with their initial act of coercion and theft. It allows them to accumulate their wealth, first in terms of piles of gold and then in the shape of numbers on ledgers and on computers.

They use this money to protect and extend their ill-gotten power, by paying individuals to physically enforce their power, paying individuals to lie on their behalf and by constructing all the machineries of their permanent domination over the majority.

Usury, loaning money at excessive rates of interest, allows those with control over the issuing of money to accumulate massive amounts of financial wealth, with the attendant accumulated power inexorably expanding towards the point of complete monopoly or complete implosion.

* * *

The writing tablets of the earliest states, which recorded details of human capital and their work credits, were just as much tools of oppression as the shackles and clubs with which the slave-labourers were bound and beaten.

But all these represent just the first components in an enormously complex composite tool for domination which has progressively taken over every aspect of our lives.

Watsuji describes how the ancient Greek civilization depended on the use of slaves and the import of foreign workers, along with wealth gained from trading: "In this way the life of the polis was more and more centred on *artificial and technical* activities which maintained its domination of the Mediterranean".[47]

He goes on to discuss Roman aqueducts, whose construction represented "nothing other than a *victory over the constraints of nature*".[48] Thanks to its aqueducts, he says, the city of Rome was able to swell to a size unthinkable for the Greeks, the people who had shown the Romans how to artificially conquer nature.

It is important to note here that the Roman aqueducts, like the Greeks' earlier achievements, served primarily to expand the power of their empire. They came into being as tools of empire, the everyday conveniences they brought to the imperial population being secondary to that overriding historical imperative.

Roszak identifies a "clear and simple political agenda" behind the contemporary continuation of these early artificial and technical activities: "to concentrate more profit and power in the hands of those who already have profit and power".[49]

French philosopher Jacques Ellul uses the term '*technique*' to describe what most would term 'technology', on the basis that the '-ology' suffix applies to the study of a subject rather than to the subject matter itself. Because the English word 'technique' has other meanings, the German term '*Technik*', much loved by the industrialist Nazis, better conveys his sense.

"We can say, taking a general view, that we have some historical experience of the choices on offer when Technik is involved. And we can see that each time, in every circumstance, Technik has always historically led us in the direction of the centralization and concentration of power",[50] says Ellul.

Right from the start, Technik's machines have been about increasing profit. "The more a business is 'productive' and competitive the less human labour it employs",[51] he notes.

"Despite attempts to demonstrate otherwise, the 'new machines' are machines to economise on the workforce. We see growing investment in capital and decreasing investment in the workforce, at the same time as the number of workers shrinks".[52]

Writing about the trend to online education, Roszak comments that this is a question of "selling a labor-saving machine in an economy where that labor is abundant and could be had for a decent wage".[53]

Human interests always come second in a society ruled by Technik. "The machine never stops", Ellul says, and to achieve maximum profitability "people have to be organised to work the same way!"[54]

Technological dependence is motivated by "obvious commercial reasons",[55] Roszak accurately remarks. Technik is a tool invented to achieve a certain aim – the increase of a minority's profit and power at the expense of the majority. Any society which takes Technik into its hands will always find itself carrying out the insidious work for which this tool was designed.

As Ellul points out, it is therefore not true to imagine that Technik is "neutral" and that its value depends on the use we make of it.[56]

Its goals, explains Roszak, have long since been selected by those who invented it, who have guided it and financed it at every point along the way in its development. It is "*their* machine".[57]

Their machine. *Their* tool. *Their* weapon used against the 99.9 per cent of humankind whom they regard as nothing more than fodder for the relentless expansion of *their* empire of exploitation and greed.

* * *

In 1948, French thinker Georges Bernanos

launched a scathing attack on machine-civilisation and its technology in the essay 'France Against the Robots', insisting: "The Civilization of the Machines is the civilization of quantity opposed to that of quality".[58]

He warns that post-war society's obsession with productivism, consumerism and money-making is threatening humankind and its spiritual well-being, observing that "we can understand nothing about modern civilisation if we don't first accept that it is a universal conspiracy against all kinds of interior life".[59]

Bernanos' analysis is well summarised by Jacques Allaire: "*Having* has replaced *being*. In our modern societies, blinded by the speed with which they can produce, the sense of having has become the one and only sense. Having is even the essence of being".[60]

Inevitably, Bernanos' critique of industrial capitalism led to him being branded "reactionary" by the cheerleaders of Technik, but he stressed that he was not looking backward but forward, to a different kind of future.

"The rule of Money is the rule of the Old. In a world which has succumbed to the dictatorship of Profit, anyone who dares to put honour before money is automatically reduced to powerlessness. It is the spirit of youth which is rejected. The youth of the world has a choice to make between two extreme solutions: surrender or revolution".[61]

* * *

The sinister agenda of The Great Reset goes beyond the techno-horrors of genetic engineering, nanotechnology, surveillance and drone warfare.

Klaus Schwab's writing has confirmed time and time again that his technocratic fascist vision is also a twisted transhumanist one.

As I explained in 2016: "This cult, which originated in the USA in the 1950s, basically envisages that humans will soon outgrow the restrictions of their natural bodies and, thanks to technological advances, evolve into semi-robotic beings. They will have artificial bodies, with replaceable parts, and their brains will eventually be uploaded into computers, giving them unimagined mental powers".[62]

Schwab's Fourth Industrial Revolution aims to merge us with machines in "curious mixes of digital-and-analog life".[63] Our bodies will be infected by nanotechnology and our privacy and freedom entirely abolished.

* * *

Roszak describes how in the USA in the 1970s, personal computers came to be seen "as a technology of liberation",[64] and elements of this

71

techno-romanticism still linger amongst those who otherwise position themselves against the dominant system (such as in the promotion of blockchain-based crypto-currencies as a form of resistance).

But the harsh reality is, as he says, that "information technology is an outgrowth of the existing industrial system"[65] and an integral part of "the ongoing military-industrial drive toward rationalizing, disciplining, and ultimately dehumanizing the workplace".[66]

Since its very beginning, IT was a collaboration between big corporations like IBM, Digital Equipment, and Data General, and the Pentagon's Defense Advanced Projects Agency (DARPA).[67] As Michael Bywater noted in *The Observer* back in 1985: "Artificial intelligence is a two-word phrase which makes US Department of Defense officials salivate when they hear it".[68]

It has long been bound up with what Roszak terms "an obsessive need to keep track of everybody's least significant movement"[69] and an accumulation of data which amounts to "a strategy of social control".[70]

Today we have reached the point where, as researcher Alison McDowell[71] has been at pains to warn us, the ruling criminal clique aims to create a digital twin of each and every one of us, herd us into smart cities, strap us with wearable technology, monitor and control our every movement and interaction, treat us as digital assets on a blockchain ledger which speculators can trade for profit.[72]

* * *

"Technik claims to liberate humanity, but in reality has set itself up as an uncontested power, which considers itself beyond judgement, escapes all democratic control, uses up natural resources and which forms within society a real 'technical system'. It threatens that which is most precious to humanity: its freedom".[73]

In thus summarising Ellul's critique, Jean-Luc Porquet also puts his finger on a key question. People generally enjoy being free and have always reacted with shudders of fear when presented with imagined dystopias involving the cold tyranny of machines and robots.

So why have we, as a society, done nothing to prevent the rise of Technik to the very brink of a Fourth Industrial Revolution designed to crush for ever the free human spirit?

The answer is simple. We have fallen for its falsehoods. As Ellul puts it: "The technological narrative is above all a narrative of lies".[74]

These lies are applied to various products of Technik. Using not just straight-forward advertising, but also the disguised marketing conveyed through TV series, films, magazine articles and newspaper reports, it tells us that the objects it has manufactured are not just highly desirable but useful to the extent that we will henceforth not be able to live without them.

They are all "solutions" to problems which, for hundreds of thousands of years, human beings had somehow never even identified.

Fridges, vacuum cleaners, cars and TVs all became "necessities" of our lives in the 20th century, in the same way that computers, internet connections and smart phones have done so in recent decades.

Behind this is a general sense of what Roszak calls "technophilia, our love affair with the machine in our lives",[75] whether that machine be a steam engine or a drone.

And this technophilia is part of a broader cult of Progress, which regards all technological innovation and sophistication as necessarily a step in a positive direction for humankind, a further advance towards an end goal which remains strangely elusive but nevertheless somehow desirable.

The myth of Progress aims to cement Technik into our lives by insisting that everything that it has done so far was good and necessary, that we could not possibly imagine our lives today without it and that the future will inevitably consist of an infinite extension of its power and activities.

Like the aristocrats of old, today's techno-crats consider themselves above the law, as Ellul says,[76] but also above all criticism. They have "rendered almost impossible general reflection on the world of Technik",[77] Porquet points out.

Technik presents itself as morally good and thereby can depict any challenge to its domination as morally bad. In the emotive, dishonest and toxic tones so typically used by defenders of the dominant system, anyone who fundamentally attacks modernity and its so-called Progress is not just misguided but dangerous, evil, threatening the very lives of those who look to Technik to prop up their existences.

The industrial system declares itself "too important to be called into question",[78] says Ellul. "No judgement is admissible which could risk standing in the way of Science or Technik".[79]

It is not considered legitimate to counter the machine-logic of Technik with concerns about the ethical value of its activities, since it is regarded as self-evident that technological advance is *always* a good thing.

Writes Ellul: "When it's a question of the dangers, costs, and so on, the scientist or technician, who has run out of arguments, closes down the discussion with 'In any case, we can't stand in the way of progress'. There is thus something here which is absolute, unassailable, against which we can do absolutely nothing, which human beings must simply obey".[80]

Technik stands radically opposed to human withness, our natural belonging to each other and to our world. It aims to replace our cultures with its own sterile uniformity.

Its much-vaunted scientific "objectivity" and "neutrality" reflect nothing but its own ethical and intellectual emptiness.

"There is no philosophy of Technik because it has nothing to do with wisdom",[81] says Ellul. "Technik is nothing other than Power".[82]

We are "indisputably in a society made entirely by and for Technik",[83] he insists, to which we are forced to submit by what he terms "a sort of state terrorism"[84] and the establishment of what is effectively "dictatorship".[85]

* * *

"As the futurologists and their political disciples present it, the rise of the information economy in America is a matter of manifest industrial destiny, a change so vast and inevitable that it might almost be a natural process beyond human control. It is hardly that. The conversion to high tech has been the result of deliberate choices on the part of our political and corporate leadership. To begin with, it was intimately linked to the steady militarization of our economic life since the beginning of World War II",[86] writes Roszak.

He warns that "something very big, new, and threatening is permeating our political life" using information technology as its tool: "What we confront in the burgeoning surveillance machinery of our society is not a value-neutral technological process; it is, rather, the social vision of the Utilitarian philosophers at last fully realized in the computer. It yields a world without shadows, secrets or mysteries, where everything has become a naked quantity".[87]

Edgar Morin identifies this very big something as "a mega-machine run by an international elite of bosses, managers, experts, economists".[88]

Ellul describes it variously as "the techno-military-state complex"[89] and "this scientific-state-techno-economical complex".[90]

Identifying the many contradictions and difficulties involved in maintaining this system, he asks how it can be kept functioning and expanding.

He replies: "In truth, there is one way, but only one: the most totalitarian global dictatorship that could ever exist".[91]

* * *

Millions of people across the world have been shocked by the ultra-authoritarian technocratic and transhumanist agenda unveiled to the public in the form of the Great Reset.

But this has been brewing for a long time, with Roszak, for instance, warning well before the turn of the century that "powerful corporate interests are at work shaping a new social order".[92]

In fact, we could say that what is happening today was an inevitability, given the way that the tyranny of Technik has been allowed to grow and grow towards this stage of suffocating domination, like a huge malignant tumour consuming the living flesh of humankind and the wider organic reality with which we are naturally one.

* * *

... What have we to do
But stand with empty hands and palms turned upwards
In an age which advances progressively backwards?

T.S. Eliot[93]

* * *

There is an overwhelming amount of evidence available today detailing the many ways in which Technik, backed by its cult of Progress, is defiling life.

Indeed, as I wrote in 2013, we do not even need officially-stamped "scientific" proof to show us that it is having a serious effect: "How could it *not*? How could it be that all these factories, power stations, processing plants, roads, airports, mines, quarries, oil wells, mills, shafts and chimneys would *not* present a serious threat to the natural world?"[94]

But the ill effects of industrial and technical development go deeper than the physical level and have corroded human society, culture and thinking.

"Life loses all its depth, beauty and tenderness, leaving only a mechanised existence",[95] writes Watsuji of our modern age. "Thousands of young men the world over are breaking their heads in vain against the iron walls of society like trapped birds in cages",[96] says Sarvepalli Radhakrishnan.

Individuals are ripped apart from any sense of withness and spellbound by Technik – "mesmerized by the multiplication of images, the intensity of noise, the dispersal of information"[97] as Ellul puts it.

This process starts from a very early age, meaning that the evolution and development of authentic and innate human qualities are stifled by this external world of shallow artifice.

Roszak warned us decades ago of future schools "where ranks of solitary students in private cubicles sit in motionless attendance upon computer terminals, their repertory of activities scaled down to a fixed stare and the repetitive stroking of a keyboard".[98]

"There will never be a machine that leaves us wiser or better or freer than our own naked mind can make us,"[99] he says.

Musing on Technik's assault on our liberty, Roszak writes: "I found myself haunted by the image of the prisoner who has been granted complete freedom to roam the 'microworld' called jail: 'Stay inside the wall, follow the rules, and you can do whatever you want'".[100]

"How far will the suppression of individual freedom go?"[101] asks Ellul and his question is all the more pertinent in the New Normal of the 2020s.

* * *

The English poet and artist William Blake was famously appalled by the "dark Satanic Mills" which blighted "England's green & pleasant land".[102]

In the new infrastructures of Technik, he saw:

turrets & towers & domes
Whose smoke destroy'd the pleasant gardens,

& whose running kennels
Chok'd the bright rivers.[103]

But his disgust reached beyond the purely physical into the whole way of thinking which made industrialism possible.

Roszak says that "Blake was among the first to link scientific sensibility to the killing pressure of the new industrial technology upon the landscape".[104]

Kathleen Raine writes: "For Blake, outward events and circumstances were the *expressions* of states of minds... Man has made his machines in the image of his ideology".[105]

Blake uses the term "single vision" to describe the system's mechanistic worldview – the "enemy of life" in Raine's words.[106]

He regards this narrowing of the intellect as nothing less than a spiritual enslavement of the people, turning them into docile wage-slaves in the new factories.

For Blake, all the many social evils that he sees around him are aspects of one vast problem, a civilization in which "Human Thought is crush'd beneath the iron hand of Power".[107]

* * *

Joseph Beuys warns that in a world ruled by Technik "ultimately perception of the interconnectedness, of the whole web of interrelationships, is destroyed".[108]

Our participation in society is hindered by the hierarchical structures within which we are all imprisoned: "Even if someone wishes to, he can't take real responsibility for his actions since everything is, as it were, done from above downwards".[109]

"Cars, for example, production methods, the capitalist way of dealing with money etc, all push into our lives. Everything of this sort, which is foisted on us, appears to be the reality, the only way of doing things, because the ability to perceive the inner substance of things is lacking".[110]

Volker Harlan, exploring Beuys' thinking, observes that just as the mechanistic modern mindset "sees the human heart as a pump, the brain as a control apparatus, it also sees humanity as something that can be centrally controlled: power control centres. Since this view sees life processes, in principle, as all repetitions of the same process, it produces bureaucratically categorized mediocrity by means of a mass psychology that negates human dignity".[111]

Beuys complains that people do not ask themselves how human society should be structured and have "no sense or perception of the archetype, that is, of the healthy condition of a social organism as it evolves".[112]

As a consequence, the social organism is "so

ill that it is absolutely high time to subject it to radical treatment, otherwise humanity will go under".[113]

* * *

The Situationist, and particularly Post-Situationist, movement in Europe has been particularly astute in its observations on modernity and industrialism.

Guy Debord, its leading figure, repeatedly explained that the dominant "spectacle" was nothing less than the commercialisation of the world, its reduction to the empty level of product and profit.

"The spectacle is the moment when the commodity has achieved the total occupation of social life",[114] he writes.

"There remains nothing, in culture or in nature, which has not been transformed, and polluted, according to the means and interests of modern industry".[115]

This industrial society is a dead thing, according to Debord, "the concrete inversion of life".[116]

After the Situationist International was dissolved in 1972, his thinking took an increasingly anti-modern and anti-industrial direction.

Patrick Marcolini observes that in Debord's

1978 film *In girum imus nocte et consumimur igni* and then in *Commentaires sur la société du spectacle*, his "romantic critique of modernity" was particularly evident, along with "a secret nostalgia for bygone times".[117]

Miguel Amorós, a jailed veteran of the Spanish resistance to Francoism who found exile in France, was involved in producing the anti-industrial *Encyclopédie des Nuisances*, a journal and then publishing house.

He writes: "Our critique of science, technology and the industrial system is a critique of progress. And in the same way it is a critique of the ideologies of science and progress, not least the workerist ideology, in both reformist and revolutionary guise, which is based on taking over, in the name of the proletariat, the bourgeois industrial system and its technology".[118]

Jaime Semprun, also involved in the *Encyclopédie des Nuisances*, regarded the notion of Progress as merely "a product of the bourgeois industrial age",[119] explains Marcolini.

Technology and science carried no promise of liberation – "on the contrary they form part of the structures of domination which have to be brought down".[120]

* * *

84

Radical poet and artist William Morris said in his first public lecture in 1878: "Everything made by man's hands has a form, which either must be beautiful or ugly; beautiful if it is in accord with Nature, and helps her; ugly if it is discordant with Nature, and thwarts her; it cannot be indifferent".[121]

Beauty is nothing other than withness made visible, whether in nature or in human beings, our works and our thought.

Anything based on the toxic anti-values of separation, self-interest, exploitation, slavery, domination and greed, anything and anyone fundamentally bad, can never transmit beauty.

As Ellul insists: "Everywhere, Technik creates ugliness".[122]

* * *

Peter Ackroyd, in his biography of Eliot, writes that the 20th century Anglo-American had "a clairvoyant sense of his time".[123]

He had become increasingly concerned by the qualitative decline of the society in which he lived and "in particular the signal inability of liberal democracy to sustain moral or intellectual values which might effectively confront the ideologies of fascism or communism",[124] says Ackroyd.

"He described the fatal weaknesses of Western democracy, and how the progress of industrialization was creating an apathetic citizenry – the kind of people who could only be aroused by despots like Hitler".[125]

Writing in 1948, Eliot argues: "We can assert with some confidence that our own period is one of decline; that the standards of culture are lower than they were fifty years ago; and that the evidences of this decline are visible in every department of human activity. I see no reason why the decay of culture should not proceed much further, and why we may not even anticipate a period, of some duration, of which it is possible to say that it will have *no* culture".[126]

Ackroyd explains that the poet had "witnessed in his lifetime the beginnings of the disintegration of European culture"[127] and saw the sources of that disintegration as lying much deeper than the political level usually cited.

He was unhappy to have found himself, initially in his native USA, living in "a society which offered no living or coherent tradition, a society being created by industrialists and bankers, and by the politics and the religion which ministered to them".[128]

Eliot wrote in 1939: "We are being made aware that the organization of society on the principle of private profit, as well as public destruction, is leading both to the deformation of humanity by unregulated industrialism, and to the exhaustion of natural resources, and that a good deal of our material progress is a progress for which succeeding generations may have to pay dearly... For a long enough time we have believed in nothing but the values arising in a mechanized, commercialized, urbanized way of life".[129]

At the end of the Second World War, Eliot's "sense of the spiritual degeneration of English life"[130] led him to fear that victory over Hitler might lead only to a post-war world based on the very same concepts of "efficiency"[131] and "material organization"[132] which had motivated the industrialist and productivist Nazi regime.

"There was a prospect ahead of 'centuries of barbarism' which in an interview the year before [1945] he had already related to the coming dominance of technology,"[133] explains Ackroyd.

"We might get a 'totalitarian democracy'", Eliot warns with remarkable foresight, "a state of affairs in which we shall have regimentation and conformity, without respect for the needs of the individual soul; the puritanism of a hygienic reality in the interest of efficiency; uniformity of opinion through propaganda and art only encouraged when it flatters the official doctrines of the time".[134]

* * *

McDowell's *Wrench in the Gears* website has shed light in recent years on the "gamification" of technology and the way in which younger generations are being tricked into helping to build the digital cages in which their lives will be imprisoned and financially exploited under the Fourth Industrial Revolution.

Ellul, who died in 1994, saw this coming. "What could be more ideal than to learn by playing?"[135] he asked, identifying the threat of "the mutation of the intelligence of the child"[136] by "the most terrorist education system in existence".[137]

"I am firmly convinced that this whole system of games, leisure and technical distraction is one of the most dangerous factors for human beings and tomorrow's society. It is that which leads us into unreality", he warned, "making us live in a totally falsified world".[138]

* * *

"Historical humankind has been mesmerized by the narrative of progress",[139] writes Scott, echoing Ellul, and his own research shows that the same is true of the narrative of the state.

The principal myth by which we are misled is that, during the long history of humankind, state control has been the norm.

The first states to emerge were "minuscule

affairs both demographically and geographi-
cally... a mere smudge on the map of the ancient
world," Scott writes. Far from representing the
global status quo, these states were "tiny nodes
of power surrounded by a vast landscape
inhabited by nonstate peoples".[140]

This remained true for thousands of years.
States were very much the exception and most of
the world's population continued to live outside
their grasp.

"In much of the world there was no state at
all until quite recently", he writes. "Outside their
reach were great congeries of 'unadministered'
peoples assembled in what historians might call
tribes, chiefdoms, and bands. They inhabited
zones of no sovereignty or vanishingly weak,
nominal sovereignty".[141]

Our understanding of this reality has long
been skewed by the fact that only states, with
their cities, monuments and written records,
tend to leave behind evidence which can later be
discovered by archaeologists and historians.

The life-without-state which existed for long
periods over large expanses of the Earth left
"little or nothing in the way of records", explains
Scott.[142]

Rather than regarding such societies as
periods of disintegration and disorder in between
the rise and fall of glorious state civilizations, we
might regard them as the natural condition from

which humankind has occasionally deviated.

But to do so would be to break the taboo by which the existence of a state is presented as an absolutely necessary pre-condition for any kind of decent human existence.

The second myth which props up the alleged "need" for a state is that they are "legitimate", along with the laws drawn up to create this impression by those who run the state, and, as a more recent extension, legitimate because they are "democratic".

I am not sure how, after the last two years, anyone could still believe that we live in anything like a democracy. As I wrote in 'Ten Things We Have Learned During the Covid Coup': "Democracy is a sham. It has been a sham for a very long time. There will never be any real democracy when money and power amount to the same thing".[143]

Ellul highlighted, as the great political illusion regarding the state, the belief "that the citizen could, through political means, master or control this state, or change it".[144]

Eliot expands on his warning of "totalitarian democracy" by describing the falsehood which surrounds our understanding of our "Western" world.

"The current terms in which we describe our society, the contrasts with other societies by which we – of the 'Western Democracies' –

eulogize it, only operate to deceive and stupify us," he observes.

"We conceal from ourselves the unpleasant knowledge of the real values by which we live. We conceal from ourselves, moreover, the similarity of our society to those which we execrate".[145]

* * *

Ellul writes that the latest manifestation of Technik is leading us into "a universe of diversion and illusion"[146] even more sophisticated and misleading than the Spectacle which had previously been described by Debord and his fellow Situationists.

Truth and reality are not just hidden from us, and replaced with false versions, but often even totally inverted by the language of a system based upon layer and layer of hypocrisy and lies.

"In any given society, the *more* they talk about a value, a virtue, a collective project", he explains, "the more *it is the sign of its absence. They talk about it precisely because the reality is the opposite*".[147]

By this handy rule of thumb, says Ellul, we can see that the real world in which we live is the complete inversion of humanism, the value constantly invoked by "liberal democracies".

At the time of writing, the system and its

propaganda cannot stop talking about "sustainability" and "saving the planet".

This is, of course, because it represents the complete inversion of all these fine-sounding words.

Rather than trying to justify the acceleration of environmental destruction represented by its Fourth Industrial Revolution, or even attempting to play down the adverse effects, it opts for the big lie of claiming that its plans are actually aimed at benefiting nature!

The idea that Technik has now somehow separated itself from its physical reality and become a "clean" and "smart" tool aimed at protecting the natural world is, of course, absurd.

Roszak spells it out: "An industrial economy is fundamentally a manufacturing economy; high tech itself requires manufacturing... A high tech economy remains a manufacturing economy if the factories have been automated".[148]

American feminist and environmental activist Judi Bari saw through power's fake green lies, declaring: "This system cannot be reformed. It is based on the destruction of the earth and the exploitation of the people.

"There is no such thing as green capitalism, and marketing cutesy rainforest products will not bring back the ecosystems that capitalism must destroy to make its profits. This is why I believe that serious ecologists must be revolutionaries".[149]

Post-Situationist Semprun warns, with René Riesel, that "precisely the same intellectual and material means used to build this world threatened with ruin, this teetering edifice, are now being deployed to diagnose the problem and recommend a remedy".[150]

Semprun died in 2010, before "climate capitalism" raised the art of greenwashing to new levels of duplicity, but had astutely predicted that "the illusion-merchants have happy days ahead of them. During the disaster, the selling goes on".[151]

Canadian investigative journalist Cory Morningstar has probably done more than anyone to expose the deceit behind the corporate "solutions" being promoted to the "climate crisis" – a narrow term which usefully renders invisible the broader environmental damage wrought by Technik.

She writes: "What is being created is a mechanism to unlock approximately 90 trillion dollars for new investments and infrastructure".[152] And she warns: "This project, of unparalleled magnitude, is the vehicle to save the failing global capitalist economic system and bring in the financialization of nature".[153]

This new infrastructure will, of course, not be in the least bit "sustainable", whatever those selling it might claim. As Ellul rightly remarks:

"Pollution will continue to develop along with the growth of Technik".[154] Or, in Morningstar's words: "This we know: the planet will not be saved by those that have destroyed it".[155]

* * *

The same falsehood, the same fake environmentalism, is currently being used to promote and justify a global land grab.

Variously termed a "New Deal for Nature" or "Nature Positive", it hides its ruthless imperialism behind the flimsy facade of "conservationism".

In his 2020 book on this "green" colonialism, Guillaume Blanc says that corporate control is being imposed on Africa under the deeply contradictory watchword of "giving nature to the people; preventing the people from living in it".[156]

He explains that this always works in more or less the same way. International conservation "experts" claim that they are working for the good of humanity, fighting poverty, hunger and disease, and so on, and that their projects are sustainable, community-based and participative.

Additionally, the love of nature felt by so many in Europe and North America is instrumentalised, by presenting a false picture of Africa as a natural paradise threatened by the presence of its own indigenous human inhabitants.

The withness of African people to their milieu is disregarded, their symbiotic relationship to the land depicted as some kind of contamination.

Once more, the hypocrisy of the system reaches the point of outright inversion of reality.

African peasant farmers, who produce their own food, very rarely buy new clothes, move around on foot and don't own computers or smart phones, are accused of "destroying nature".

But in fact, as Blanc points out: "If we want to save the planet, we should be living like them".[157]

* * *

I have recently written a lot about the fake left and its response to the Great Reset coup. This has gone beyond mere lack of resistance to outright support of authoritarian measures and vitriolic smearing of those who dare challenge them.

The seeds of this betrayal were, however, sown back in the 19th century when socialism embraced two of the system's primary tools of oppression – the state and Technik.

The new Marxist orthodoxy banished the old socialist dream of a better future, now condemned as hopelessly "utopian", in favour of a red-tinted version of the dominant system's own cult of Progress.

Furthermore, it actually defined the human beings it claimed to represent in terms of the servile role they were being forced to carry out under that same system.

It therefore no doubt seemed quite natural to these "workers" that after the Bolshevik Revolution they would continue to spend their lives working, sacrificing their own freedom and happiness for the "greater good" of progressive industrialism.

Liberalism is also a misleading political position in that it never expresses any real principled commitment to the democratic principles it likes to flaunt, insisting ultimately on the need for "law and order" to protect the profitable infrastructures of its economy from popular disorder.

It represents, as I have written elsewhere, "the two-faced tyranny of wealth"[158] which can easily switch into authoritarian mode whenever it sees fit, whether in the 1920s and 1930s or in the 2020s.

That is not to say, of course, that the values *superficially* represented by political liberalism would not be laudable if they were genuine.

The problem lies in the gap between this representation (the blurb on the cover) and the toxic reality that it masks – along with the apparent inability of modern citizens to distinguish one from the other.

Again and again we can see genuine people attached to a political ideology or movement because they believe it is what it *claims* to be – a struggle to save the planet, to bring about social justice, to defend decency or whatever.

While they, and their good intentions, are not themselves fake, they *reinforce fakeness* by gullibly accepting as authentic the slick PR image presented by movements which are in fact being used for completely different, usually exactly opposite, purposes.

They act innocently, perhaps, but stupidly, like someone who allows their judgement to be constantly swayed by advertising or who easily falls prey to con-artists or fraudsters.

We can see this phenomenon in action with historical Fascism and Nazism. On the surface, these allied movements in Italy and Germany stood up for "the people", both in terms of the nation, *Das Volk*, and in terms of the idealised majority of hard-working ordinary citizens whose interests they were supposed to represent.

But fascism, like Marxism, not only failed to escape from the trap of regarding the state and Technik as essential for human existence, but worshipped them as the foundations of its new order.

Behind its lip service to its "people" lay a

dehumanising ideology of unrestrained productivism and industrialism that regarded them as nothing but fodder for the machineries of profit which these authoritarian regimes really served.

Anyone who digs a little into fascism will quickly discover that, like Technik in general, it has no real philosophy.

There is plenty of stirring rhetoric and use of ideas and imagery designed to attract fanatical support for a limited period of time, but all of this lacks essential coherence and has no depth or soul.

It is telling that Eliot, who "seemed too radical to conservatives and too conservative to radicals",[159] was not ultimately drawn to fascism (as his friend Ezra Pound sadly was) finding that it "it could not provide any set of objective values or principles".[160]

* * *

Sister, mother
And spirit of the river, spirit of the sea
Suffer me not to be separated

And let my cry come unto Thee

T.S. Eliot[161]

* * *

The falsehood oozing from every pore of modern society is not confined to the detail of the particular instances above; there is a general sense of disconnection from authentic reality.

Ironically, this departure from truth seems to be connected to a long-term obsession with "facts".

Roszak traces this phenomenon back to the 17th century when, he says, scientific thinkers became so suspicious of ideas which had become fixed dogma that they called into question the very validity of *ideas*.

"They recommended a new point of departure, one which seemed innocuously neutral and therefore strategically inoffensive to the cultural authorities of the day: they would concentrate their attention on the clear-cut indisputable facts of common experience – the weights and sizes and temperatures of things. Facts first, they insisted. Ideas later".[162]

This historic departure from traditional wisdom has had serious consequences, believes Radhakrishnan: "We are slaves of a mechanical system of ideas. Rationalist codes of morality sacrifice flexibility and richness to correctness and consistency. Professing to act on principles, our intellectuals are cut off from the deeper sources of vitality and their souls are at strife with their minds".[163]

By the early 1960s, notes Roszak, it became commonplace for people to speak of their minds as being "programmed", revealing that "people were coming to see themselves more and more as a kind of machine: a biocomputer".[164]

As a result we find ourselves in a culture in which "the mind in all its aspects can now be been as 'nothing but' a rather complicated information-shuffling machine that works up its highest powers from simple, formal procedures that organize data points".[165]

This mechanistic "scientific" outlook ignores the organic reality of human beings, describing us as if we were artificially-manufactured machines rather than extensions of the living flesh of nature.

This is simply not true! It is yet another falsehood propping up the system.

Just as our bodies are the fruit of nature, so is our thinking. As we saw in Part I, our minds are formed and informed by the patterns which make up the underlying order of the cosmos, which emerge in our consciousness as archetypes, myths and ideas.

"The mind thinks with ideas, not with information",[166] stresses Roszak. "Only one narrow band of our experience is represented in the computer: logical reason. Sensual contact, intuition, inarticulated common-sense judgments, aesthetic taste have been largely, if not wholly, left out. We do not bring the full resources of the self to the computer".[167]

It is absurd, he says, to pretend that "artificial intelligence" can interpret reality in the same way as the human mind: "Interpretation belongs solely to a living mind in exactly the same way that birth belongs solely to a living body. Disconnected from a mind, 'interpretation' becomes what 'birth' becomes when it does not refer to a body: a metaphor".[168]

Any digital interpretation or representation, such as the virtual digital world proposed under the Fourth Industrial Revolution, can never be anything than a "rough caricature"[169] of reality, he says.

The understanding of humanity, life and the cosmos presented to us by Technik and its fragmented machine-thinking is a sub-standard replica, a cheap pixelated substitute for authenticity.

It can provide us with no understanding of human beings or our withness to the world in which we live.

Augustin Berque identifies an early denial of our natural *médiance* in the *Discours de la methode* of his compatriot René Descartes, where the influential 17th century philosopher announces that he has no need of any place[170] in which to carry out the thinking which he famously claims proves his existence ("I think therefore I am").

"What he means, is that he is himself by means of himself, independently of everything around him. This is a radical break with traditional notions, which always saw people as connected to their milieu".[171]

This outlook, which became dominant, extracted the human subject from nature, from the world, and depicted him as some kind of separate observer who was not actually part of the reality in which he lived.

It is not only false but dangerous for our well-being.

Berque explains that it means we lose our bearings in our individual existence, that we become incapable of feeling a real connection between our interior world and the outside world, "between the microcosm (the little world which concerns you personally) and the macrocosm (the big world of the universe, nature and humanity)".[172]

The idea of a totally objective point of view, a point of view from an abstract nowhere, is nonsensical since, as Berque remarks, "living beings are always situated somewhere, in a certain milieu".[173]

While in recent decades the notion of objectivity has been rejected by scientists, particularly in the realm of quantum physics, the mindset of which it forms part has continued to pollute general thinking.

In his 2018 book *Le Sens des limites: contre l'abstraction capitaliste*, Renaud Garcia argues that the artificiality and abstraction of life under Technik is depriving us of a real sense of being alive – in our bodies, in our daily lives, in our milieu: "In this world of artifice, going beyond the surface to a deeper level, that of the sheer essence of things, is no longer conceivable".[174]

He condemns transhumanism, which he says "reduces the human brain to a simple processor of information, a mere calculating machine"[175] and is built on the "basic negation of the reality of living organisms".[176]

* * *

"As European cities grew and forested areas became more remote, as fens were drained and geometric patterns of channels imposed on the landscape, as large powerful waterwheels, furnaces, forges, cranes, and treadmills began increasingly to dominate the work environment, more and more people began to experience nature as altered and manipulated by machine technology",[177] writes Carolyn Merchant in *The Death of Nature*.

"A slow but unidirectional alienation from the immediate daily organic relationship that had formed the basis of human experience from earliest times was occurring. Accompanying these changes were alterations in both the theories and experiential bases of social organization which had formed an integral part of the organic cosmos".[178]

With the industrial age, supported by its dogma of fakeness, separation and fragmentation, we have, in George Lapierre's words, "broken the primordial pact" and "we are paying the price for this on every level: social disintegration, spiritual blindness, disruption of the cosmic environment. Human life is going to become impossible".[179]

Radhakrishnan saw the same thing happening back in 1929: "Since the primaeval unity is broken, man is uncertain and wavering. We seem to be alienated from nature, leading sceptical, artificial and self-centred lives".[180]

Berque is right when he says that the links between a person and their milieu, or indeed with nature itself, can never be suppressed,[181] but *awareness* of these links *can* be severely eroded.

"A sense of the basic emotional unity between man and the moods and forms of Nature" is, as William Anderson observes, an idea "foreign to the dominant scientific and cultural philosophies".[182]

For those who are intent on building a

world-prison based on our separation from each other and from nature, widespread awareness of withness represents an obstacle to their nefarious "progress".

Robert Graves laments that for the modern town-dweller, "the one variety of religion acceptable to him is a logical, ethical, highly abstract sort which appeals to his intellectual pride and sense of detachment from wild nature".[183]

People who have spent their lives amongst brick and concrete are no longer capable of understanding the sense of age-old wisdom and culture rooted in our belonging to the Earth, he laments. "The commonest references to natural phenomena in traditional poetry, which was written by countrymen for countrymen, are becoming unintelligible".[184]

Roszak notes that this breach with nature, and thus with reality, very much suits the purposes of those who promote the urban-industrial system, "hoping to see it mature into a wholly new order of life in which science and technology have permanently mastered the forces of nature and have undertaken to redesign the planet".[185]

There is a downward spiral involved here. The more we are physically separated from nature, the less we care about it and the easier it becomes for the criminal profiteers to plunder and destroy the organism to which we (unknowingly!) belong.

It is hard not to join Eliot in sensing in this modern world "the presence of evil and darkness"[186] and in feeling the advent of "the dark ages".[187]

Today, we are faced with what Berque calls a "third stage"[188] of separation from our withness, in a world of transhumanism and geo-engineering of which shameless artifice is the jealous god.

Disorientated, disembodied and dispossessed by power and its endless lies, we stumble further still from the Withway.

PART III: FINDING THE WITHWAY

Pleasure cannot be ours as long as we wander from the true path of mankind. In your heart, therefore, seek the true path and then the pleasure shall be added.

Kaibara Ekken[1]

* * *

As we saw in Part II, the root cause of our separation lies in the power which has been accumulated by a criminal ruling clique.

The classic form taken by this violent and thieving entity is the state, but it uses other guises. When states expand they become empires. When an empire has expanded to embrace everything, everywhere, it has become a global tyranny.

Whatever name power gives to its physical structure – nation, union of nations or world order – this will always be a weapon wielded, from above, against the people. The bigger and more powerful this weapon, the wider the control it can exert and the greater the damage it can inflict.

Our first priority in rediscovering our withness will therefore have to be a rejection of this power and its vehicles of oppression.

If this rejection happened in stages, the first stage would necessarily be a decentralization of power from the global level at which it is currently exercised.

But we can't stop there. The decentralization has to go right down through the whole of society to the extent that it amounts to a reversal in the *direction* of power.

Instead of power imposed on those below by those above, we would see power emerging from the grassroots in the shape of an *empowerment* which resists all attempts to control and exploit.

We have to see through the lie that we are incapable of running our own lives and communities in the way that we see fit, forget any notion that our decision-making role can be safely handed over to "democratically-elected representatives".

Jacques Ellul points out that members of the political class, divided into parties which seem to be constantly at war with each other, are essentially working together to defend their class status: "And as long as supposedly democratic countries have a political class, they can *never* have any real politics and real democracy".[2]

* * *

Money is another tool of power; a tool of compliance. But it is a symbolic tool. It has no physical reality.

We cannot eat or drink money. It does not warm us in winter or shelter us from the winds. It does not carry us from one place to another, compose or perform music, make us laugh, tell us stories or make us think.

We do not *need* money. It is true that in our money-based society, certain things can only be acquired with money. But this state of affairs only reflects our collective submission to the class which invented and controls money and wields it as the weapon of its continuing domination.

Money is the suit of clothes in which the Emperor-Thief parades pompously through our lives, demanding that we applaud and grovel before his splendour.

But when, one day, a small voice calls out that he is naked and ridiculous, that his finery is make-believe, then the spell is broken. The people realise that they have been fooled and the charlatan-tyrant is run out of town to hoots of derisive laughter.

* * *

If money is merely a means, then "work" as we know it today is a *means to a means*. We have to labour to earn a wage because without money we cannot exist in the society built by the money-power.

Work, in an old-fashioned sense, always has to be done. Food has to be gathered, grown, prepared. Water has to be fetched. Homes have to be built, cleaned, maintained. Clothes and shoes and tables and knives and dishes have to be fashioned. The sick and the young and the old have to be cared for.

But this is work we do for ourselves, because it has to be done or we want to do it. It is as much a part of human existence as breathing and walking and does not keep us chained up for hour upon endless hour, for week after week, year after year, decade after decade.

Working with a knife at our throats, because a criminal mafia insists we pay for the pleasure of living in the world that they have stolen from us, does not make us free. It makes us slaves.

* * *

Power has built up an intermeshing machinery of tools with which to keep us in our profit-yielding place.

"Peasantries with long experience of on-the-ground statecraft have always understood that the state is a recording, registering, and measuring machine", writes James Scott, citing its use of conscription, forced labour, land seizures and head taxes.

"The firm identification in their minds between paper documents and the source of their oppressions has meant that the first act of many peasant rebellions has been to burn down the local records office where these documents are housed".[3]

Power is permanently afraid that its rule might collapse under the pressure of popular resistance. It tells us that the "sustainability" and "resilience" of its vile system of exploitation are of paramount importance for our well-being and depicts its potential loss of control as a nightmare scenario, the "end of civilization", a "descent into anarchy".

Time and time again throughout history, empires have collapsed and given way to societies which leave behind no official records and no archaeological evidence of awe-inspiring grandeur.

Writes Scott: "If the population remains, it is likely to have dispersed to smaller settlements and villages. Higher-order elites disappear; monumental building activity ceases; use of literacy for administrative and religious purposes is likely to evaporate; larger-scale trade and redistribution is sharply reduced; and specialist craft production for elite consumption and trade is diminished or absent. Taken together, such changes are often understood to be a deplorable regression away from a more civilized culture".[4]

But the collapse of a "typically oppressive state"[5] is less likely to mean a dissolution of a culture than its "reformulation and decentralization"[6] and need not imply a decline in human health, well-being, or nutrition, he explains.

In fact, "there is a strong case to be made that such 'vacant' periods represented a bolt for freedom by many state subjects and an improvement in human welfare".[7]

Can we imagine "the vast population not subject to state control",[8] an "intricate web of relatively egalitarian settlements"[9] peopled by "opportunistic generalists with a large portfolio of subsistence options spread across several food webs"?[10]

If we are instructed by the dogma of modernity that such a thing is simply not possible, this is no doubt because such ways of living are "environmentally resistant to centralization and control from above"[11] and "the very breadth of a subsistence web – hunting, fishing, foraging, and gathering in a variety of ecological settings – poses insurmountable obstacles to the imposition of a single political authority".[12]

*   *   *

... Round and round the fire
Leaping through the flames, or joined in circles,
Rustically solemn or in rustic laughter
Lifting heavy feet in clumsy shoes,
Earth feet, loam feet, lifted in country mirth,
Mirth of those long since under the earth
Nourishing the corn. Keeping time,
Keeping the rhythm in their dancing
As in their living in the living seasons
The time of the seasons and the constellations
The time of the milking and the time of harvest
The time of the coupling of man and woman
And that of beasts. Feet rising and falling.
Eating and drinking. Dung and death.

T.S. Eliot[13]

*   *   *

"I believe that if India, and through India the world, is to achieve real freedom, then sooner or later we shall have to go and live in the villages – in huts, not in palaces. Millions of people can never live in cities and palaces in comfort and peace",[14] wrote Mohandas Gandhi in a letter to fellow Indian independence campaigner Jawaharlal Nehru in 1945.

He argues elsewhere: "Given the demand,

there is no doubt that most of our wants can be supplied by the villages. When we become village-minded we shall not want imitations from the West or machine-made products".[15]

"My idea of village *swaraj* is that it is a complete republic, independent of its neighbours for its own vital wants, and yet inter-dependent for many others in which dependence is a necessity.

"Thus, every village's first concern will be to grow its own food crops and cotton for its clothes... My economic creed is a complete taboo in respect to all foreign commodities, whose importation is likely to prove harmful to our indigenous interests. This means that we may not in any circumstances import a commodity that can be adequately supplied from our country".[16]

One of Gandhi's closest political colleagues, Bharatan Kumarappa, wrote the book *Capitalism, Socialism or Villagism* while he was being held as a political prisoner of the occupying British regime.

Gandhi, in his foreword to this work, credits Kumarappa with inventing the word "villagism" to describe their shared vision of decentralised communities based around traditional crafts and culture.

Kumarappa explains that villagism is rooted in ancient pre-industrial ways of living and is *not* derived from Western socialism.

"The idea of social ownership of production and sharing of things in common was not original to Socialism. Such an arrangement existed in some form or other even in early times, when a whole community or village held land and other property in common and distributed wealth among its members".[17]

He is very critical of orthodox socialism for its dependence on a central state to manage its supposedly egalitarian society, warning: "As Capitalism took away wealth which rightly belonged to the people and accumulated it in the hands of the capitalist, Socialism takes away the power which rightly belongs to the people and concentrates it in the State.

"And concentration of power is not less dangerous than concentration of wealth; for men get intoxicated with power and can use it with disastrous effect against those who disagree with them".[18]

Kumarappa insists that his proposed society would act as a bulwark against all concentrations of power, on the national and international level: "We must not think of Villagism therefore as only a matter of economic arrangement but as a social order aiming at ridding the world of imperialism and war".[19]

Watsuji Tetsurô says that the Indian human being is one who "hates the obligations of life in the *polis* and who loves the independence provided by *agriculture and the communal organisation of the village*.[20]

But the Gandhian vision of withlife sourced from local autonomy has been shared by many others, not least English radical William Morris, part of the Pre-Raphaelite movement.

In his 1891 novel *News From Nowhere*, Morris "envisaged a postindustrial future that recreated the preindustrial past, a society of villages, family farms, and tribal settlements",[21] as Theodore Roszak puts it.

Austrian-Jewish philosopher Martin Buber rejected modern industrial society in favour of what he called a New Community.

In the 1900 essay 'Alte und neue Gemeinschaft', he describes how this would be based on the "living mutual action of integral human beings".

It would replace the principle of utility with the principle of creativity, allowing individuals to accomplish their human potential.

He argues: "Thus will humanity, which came out from a beautiful but rough primitive community, after going through the growing slavery of *Gesellschaft*, arrive at a new community, which will no longer be grounded, as the first one was, on blood affinities (*Blutverwandtschaft*), but on elective affinities (*Wahlverwandtschaft*)".

Only in these circumstances, insists Buber, could the age-old revolutionary utopian dream come true and "the instinctive life-unity of the primitive human being (*Urmenschen*), which has been for so long fragmented and divided, return at a higher level and in a new form".[22]

He adds elsewhere: "The new organic whole, founded on the regeneration of the 'cells' of the social tissue, will be the renaissance (rather than the return) of organic community in the shape of a decentralised federation of small communities".[23]

Universal human withlife is what T.S. Eliot describes as the traditional "norm" of a "small and mostly self-contained group attached to the soil and having its interests centred in a particular place, with a kind of unity which may be designed, but which also has to grow through generations".

He states: "It is the idea, or ideal, of a community small enough to consist of a nexus of direct personal relationships, in which all iniquities and turpitudes will take the simple and easily appreciable form of wrong relations between one person and another".[24]

Finding the Withway is rediscovering our belonging to each other and to the land where we live and we do well to pay heed to the experience of those "primal" peoples who today still preserve that wisdom.

They can tell us not only how people thought and lived in the past but also how people will have to think and live in the future.

As philosopher Tu Wei-ming affirms: "What we can learn from them, then, is a fundamental restructuring of our way of perceiving, thinking, and living; we are urgently in need of a new attitude and a new worldview".[25]

* * *

No: there seems no escape from our difficulties until the industrial system breaks down... and nature reasserts herself with grass and trees among the ruins.

Robert Graves[26]

* * *

It seems entirely evident that what we need "is nothing less than the break-up of Technik's society", as Jacques Ellul puts it in 'Autopsie de la révolution'.[27]

However, the ruling mafia have, we saw in Part II, constructed a powerful taboo against any fundamental questioning of the relentless machineries of Technik.

They have created the illusion that the advance of what they call Progress is bound up with the very passing of time, that its endless proliferation is not only desirable but pretty much inevitable, barring some kind of "disaster".

Even many of those who have accompanied us this far towards the Withway will no doubt stop short in the face of the ideological warning tape placed across our path by the system's thought police.

They will regurgitate the received opinion that turning our backs on industrialism as a whole is unrealistic, unworkable and unnecessary; that those of us who propose such a direction for humanity are extreme, deluded and even dangerous.

They prefer what they regard as the sensible, pragmatic and safe option of simply reducing the environmental damage caused by Technik, by cutting waste, recycling and making use of the latest shiny bright-green innovations manufactured by Technik itself.

But, in truth, this sensible and safer option does not exist!

Industrialism can never be sustainable, its products are always polluting, its endless cancerous growth is its permanent and essential logic.

The only other alternative to the ending of industrial Technik is the *continuation* of industrial Technik and this continuation will *inevitably* lead to two things.

Firstly, and more obviously, the natural world of which are part, including the soil which feeds us, the water we drink and the air we breathe, will be progressively polluted and degraded to a point of unimaginable misery.

Secondly, because Technik is a weapon wielded by criminal power, the vast majority of humankind will be increasingly assaulted, controlled and enslaved by its infrastructures – a process which is already accelerating at an alarming rate.

If those who reject the Withway of deindustrialisation really welcome this other option, even when its implications have been made clear to them, then they should come out and say so openly: "I hereby declare that my lazy attachment to a certain familiar sense of reality and to a largely comfortable way of life, with all the conveniences which I enjoy today, is more precious to me than the freedom of future generations and even the continuation of life on Earth".

That way, at least, we will all be able to see clearly where their priorities and values really lie. As will their children, their grandchildren and their great grandchildren, if our species survives that long...

* * *

I am part of the modern world, descended from generations of city-dwellers whose connection to nature was limited to the tending of a vegetable patch or a weekend excursion into the countryside just outside London.

I was born into a reality where there is always hot water in the taps and where a room can be lit at the flick of a switch. While I am now happy to live without fridge, washing machine or vacuum cleaner, I still listen to recorded music, make telephone calls and connect to the internet.

But the fact that I am personally inexperienced in non-industrial living does not mean that I cannot see the path that humankind *has to* now take.

If we cannot rise to a collective level of imagination that surpasses our accumulated personal habits and conditioning, we will never be able to leave behind the debased way of life in which we have been confined and we will never rediscover our natural withness and vitality.

* * *

This land of ours was once, we are told, the abode of the Gods. It is not possible to conceive Gods inhabiting a land which is made hideous by the smoke and din of mill chimneys and factories, and whose roadways are traversed by rushing engines.

Mohandas Gandhi[28]

* * *

Power has physical form in the shape of its factories, its oil refineries, its mines, its docks, its server farms, its airports, its motorways, its railways, its chemical plants, its pylons, its pipelines, its cables, its satellites, its phone masts, its surveillance cameras, its tanks, its missiles, its drones, its robots, its army bases and its prisons.

But its *real* control over us and our lives is psychological. It has persuaded us that its toxic existence and growth is completely normal, acceptable and even beneficial.

Its strength is based on the lies it tells us, the narrative with which it blinds us to the reality of what it is and what it is doing to us.

If we are ever to escape its deadly grip, and find ourselves on the Withway to a decent human future, *awareness* is therefore of utmost importance, on every level.

For instance, on a physical and biological plane we *remain* in a state of withness to the rest of humankind – it is only our *knowledge* of that belonging which is often sadly lacking.

As we have seen, ancient Chinese philosopher Mozi identified the problem, 2,400 years ago, as being the "partiality" which allowed people to enjoy a subject-to-subject relationship with members of their family or immediate community, but blinded to them to their withness with regard to strangers.

For Mozi, "the natural identification with one's own community ought to be expanded to other cities and states", explains Lawrence F. Hundersmarck.[29]

"Only when everyone regards any other as another self will all be secure".[30]

* * *

Truth is organic
It does not come down from heavens
For it rises from the earth

Clément Pansaers[31]

* * *

The great Russian writer Leo Tolstoy used the term "love" to describe this withness of the heart, this realisation that "we are all members of one great body".[32]

He did not stop short at the human level. "We are spiritually connected on all sides – not only with people but with all living creatures",[33] he declared. "Whether they know this or not, all creatures are inseparably connected".[34]

What has to be overcome is the psychological separation of the individual from the context to which they belong.

Sri Aurobindo writes that an ideal society "would respect the freedom of each of its members and maintain itself not by law and force but by the free and spontaneous consent of its constituent persons", noting that this would be difficult to create "so long as individual man clings to his egoism as the primary source of existence".[35]

This detachment from the individual ego is a practice which could be described as spiritual or mystic, but not necessarily religious in the usual sense of the term.

Orthodox religions tend, in fact, to reinforce separation – perhaps because they are, as Joseph Campbell observes, "concerned primarily with the maintenance of a certain social order".

He adds: "The mystic way, on the other hand, plunges within, to those nerve centers that are in all members of the human race alike, and are at once the well springs and ultimate receptacles of life and all experience of life".[36]

This mystic awareness of human, natural and cosmic withness has not been a prominent feature of most cultural and political movements opposing dominant power, which is perhaps why we have been so far unable to cast off the shackles of oppression.

One notable exception was the Dada movement of the early 20th century, a defiant explosion of vital creativity against the crushing cogs of industrial doom.

"Confronted by the hostility of the modern world towards mystical existences, they placed modern art and avant-garde techniques at the service of an underground transmission of a very ancient spiritual-philosophical tradition",[37] says Benjamin Hennot.

Writing about Belgian Dada-ist Clément Pansaers, he argues: "From his self-proclaimed rebirth in 1916 until his death in 1922, all his work can be seen as a contemporary European extension of the Taoist tradition and, more precisely, as a new chapter of Chuang Tzu, who isn't an author, but a 'philosophical' tradition".[38]

Pansaers and his colleagues were thus striking out in exactly the opposite direction to the Technik-worshipping avant-garde who found themselves in step with the hyper-industrialism of the fascist and communist regimes.

"For him it is not a question of allowing himself to be galvanised by the forces unleashed by industrial development, as the futurists desired, but rather of abandoning himself to the cosmogonic flow which gives rise to all beings and all things",[39] notes Hennot.

Watsuji writes about *kiai*, a harmony of vital

breath, which he says "we can only feel intuitively".[40]

Our awareness of withness, our withness-as-awareness, is there waiting for us if only we could free ourselves from the malign influence of life-hating, spirit-stifling Technik.

* * *

Most people today are not withfolk. They have, tragically, lost all awareness of their withness, all sense of their grounding in the natural texture of existence, all access to the strength of the cosmic flow within them.

As a result they are insecure, self-obsessed and fearful – ideal victims for tyrants who know how to play on these fundamental weaknesses.

"Modern man is afraid and lives in anxiety: he focuses his anxiety (provoked by the Technik surrounding him) on illness", writes Ellul.

"Modern man no longer knows how to suffer, can no longer overcome even the slightest pain. He no longer knows how to mobilise his inner resources to fight by himself against anxiety or fear".[41]

German philosopher Ernst Jünger describes in *The Forest Passage* the "gullibility of modern man" – a lack of spiritual faith lethally combined with a misplaced faith in contemporary power: "He believes what he reads in the newspaper but not what is written in the stars".[42]

He adds: "The need to hear the news several times a day is already a sign of fear; the imagination grows and paralyzes itself in a rising vortex".[43]

If regaining awareness is the key to finding the Withway, and thus escaping tyranny, then the process must necessarily begin within the individual mind.

How we might each go about achieving this is set out by Aurobindo in his inspirational metaphysical masterpiece, *The Synthesis of Yoga*.

"We have to see Life as a channel for the infinite force divine"[44] he says, and thus banish the psychologically-crippling illusion of individual separation, isolation and powerlessness.

"Truly, we do not think, will or act but thought occurs in us, will occurs in us, impulse and act occur in us; our ego-sense gathers around itself, refers to itself all this flow of natural activities. It is cosmic Force, it is Nature that forms the thought, imposes the will, imparts the impulse. Our body, mind and ego are a wave of that sea of force in action and do not govern it, but by it are governed and directed.[45]

"The Yogin is able to feel his body one with all bodies, to be aware of and even to participate in their affections; he can feel constantly the unity of all Matter and be aware of his physical being as only a movement in its movement. Still more easily yet is it possible for him to feel constantly and normally the whole sea of the infinite life as his true vital existence and his own life as only a wave of that boundless surge".[46]

Because this feeling of withness is an awareness of something which already exists, but has been forgotten, we do not need to mentally strive in order to find it, explains Aurobindo.

The seeker of the Withway gradually realises that "a force other than his own, a force transcending his egoistic endeavour and capacity, is at work in him and to this Power he learns progressively to submit himself" and "in the end his own will and force become one with the higher Power; he merges them in the divine Will and its transcendent and universal Force".[47]

But this realisation of our universal belonging is only the first stage of the process, the "turning point", as Aurobindo explains. "For now we begin to understand the sense of our struggles and efforts, successes and failures. At last we are able to seize the meaning of our ordeals and sufferings and can appreciate the help that was given us by all that hurt and resisted and the utility of our very falls and stumblings".[48]

Withness is always our reality, whether we

are aware of it or not. But when we *have* gained awareness of it, on the highest metaphysical plane, its light shines on everything else beneath, illuminating our understanding and informing our action on every level.

"We are able to become without egoism, bondage or reaction the channel in our mind and body for a divine action poured out freely upon the world",[49] Aurobindo contends.

From this new perspective, of our return to everyday life informed by our complete awareness, the significance of everything is reversed.

Instead of seeing around us a host of separate beings, objects and phenomena, and trying to piece all this together to make some sort of sense out of the apparent confusion, we start from the knowledge of unity and work down from there.

As Aurobindo writes: "The gnosis dwells in the unity and knows by it all the nature of the diversities; it starts from the unity and sees diversities only of a unity, not diversities constituting the one, but a unity constituting its own multitudes. The gnostic knowledge, the gnostic sense, does not recognise any real division; it does not treat things separately as if they were independent of their true and original oneness".[50]

Alan Fox says of the philosopher Fazang that he taught that "since all things are in causal relations with other things, their being overlaps, so to speak, and it is then wrong to conceive of things as separate or discrete".[51]

In practice, this means seeing a wood rather than a number of trees, looking for factors which unite and explain rather than divide and confuse, going beyond the apparent chaotic separation of people and phenomena and searching for the patterns, the fundamental order, that always lie beneath.

For the 11th century Cheng brothers (Cheng Hao and Cheng Yi), writes James D. Sellmann, "there are many manifestations of principle, but principle is always one. The myriad forms all constitute one body because they originate from the one principle and contain that principle".[52]

The Chinese philosopher-siblings emphasise unity, judging that the metaphysical, the ethical, the natural, the human, the mind, human nature, destiny, principle, and the self-cultivation of moral virtue are all ultimately linked together. They insist: "The highest truth is always resolved into unity, and an essential principle is never a duality".[53]

This was the age-old understanding presented in "scientific" terms by the German philosopher Georg Hegel, much misunderstood today due to the way that his thought was subsequently stripped of its metaphysical basis by one group of followers and turned to purely political ends.

With his dialectic, he was stressing that all of reality is contained within the universe as a whole: there is a general *Zusammenhang* or framing context. This means that all apparent differences can necessarily be transcended at a higher level.

Jacques d'Hondt writes that the Hegelian dialectic is "a logic of universal interdependence, of the inseparability and unity of opposites, of going beyond ruptures, a logic of becoming".[54]

And Frederick Beiser regards the dialectic as arising from Hegel's nature-based thinking and "its triadic schema of organic development, according to which organic growth consists in three moments: unity, difference and unity-in-difference".[55]

* * *

At the same time as the individual can only be understood in the context of the universal, the knowledge of that universality can only come to the individual from within his own deepest, universal, essence.

"Individualism is as necessary to the final perfection as the power behind the group-spirit; the stifling of the individual may well be the stifling of the god in man," writes Aurobindo.

"There is continually a danger that the

exaggerated social pressure of the social mass by its heavy unenlightened mechanical weight may suppress or unduly discourage the free development of the individual spirit. For man in the individual can be more easily enlightened, conscious, open to clear influences; man in the mass is still obscure, half-conscious, ruled by universal forces that escape its mastery and its knowledge".[56]

When the individual realises his power to channel and express the light of the universe, he can allow the life force which has always animated him to take on a new meaning as "an indispensable intermediary"[57] between above and below, a way of enabling the highest truth to become present and active in the physical world.

Our *awareness* of our belonging to the whole is a necessary stage in allowing us to act and live in accordance with that knowledge.

While some Eastern traditions suggest that when we have become aware of cosmic withness we should withdraw from the "illusion" of the physical reality we have previously experienced, Aurobindo's philosophy insists that, on the contrary, we should return to the fray in a renewed form.

"An absolute liberty of experience and of the restatement of knowledge in new terms and new combinations is the condition of its self-formation. Seeking to embrace all life in itself, it is in the position not of a pilgrim following the highroad to his destination, but, to that extent at least, of a path-finder hewing his way through a virgin forest".[58]

"In Life itself there is the seed of its own salvation".[59]

* * *

John Cowper Powys judges that in the face of all the "vulgar sensationalism"[60] and "commercialized opinion"[61] with which we are continually besieged in the modern world, we have to create our own personal philosophy to uphold the values which are important to us.

Ultimately this has to be sourced from within each one of us.

When you consider a cultured person's individual philosophy "you feel that this is what he has secretly and profoundly lived by for many a long year",[62] says Powys. "That this personal philosophy already exists before it is brought into conscious articulation cannot be doubted".[63]

This authentic personal philosophy has to be embedded within one's very personality and existence. "To philosophize is not to read philosophy, it is to feel philosophy",[64] Powys stresses.

"With a cultured man there is no gap or lacuna between his opinion and his life. Both are dominated by the same organic, inevitable fatality. They are what he is".[65]

* * *

Seekers of the Withway – "the thinkers, the artists and the heroes" – draw inspiration from the universal and, in doing so, suffer a superficial separation from other people, writes Sarvepalli Radhakrishnan.

"They are lonely, self-centred, not by choice but by necessity. Genius has no place for team-work. Poets and prophets do not go into committees".[66]

Radhakrishnan says that the individual who has achieved spiritual freedom has a vision of life so clear and complete that "it lives through days of darkness, beholding the sun with the eye of the soul".[67]

Such a person is sustained by his inner vision of withlife, even when this is not reflected in the society in which he lives. "He is able to face crises in life with a mind full of serenity and joy, the joy which is the sign of proper fulfilment of function, nature's seal that life's direction is right and secure".[68]

When we descend deep inside ourselves to find out who we really are, we simultaneously ascend to our essential withness and are forever transformed.

"Individuation is an at-one-ment with oneself and at the same time with humanity, since oneself is a part of humanity", writes Carl Jung.[69]

Radmila Moacanin describes it as "essentially an unconscious, autonomous process in which the psyche in its natural and spontaneous urge for wholeness is striving to harmonize its conscious and unconscious contents".[70]

She adds: "When one has become truly oneself, that unique individual – unlike anyone else who has ever lived, an unrepeatable spark in the universe – one no longer has the need for competition, for hatred and hostility, for power to dominate others; compassionate wisdom spontaneously arises".[71]

* * *

"Individuality is a thing that cannot be killed. Quietly it may be, but just as certainly, silently, perhaps, as the growth of a blade of grass, it offers its perpetual and unconquerable protest against the dictates of Authority",[72] writes American anarchist and feminist Voltairine de Cleyre.

The malign Dominant Idea stifling the human spirit can only be challenged if individuals have the courage and determination to resist its power and are able to source, and remain true to, a sense of justice that comes from within themselves, she explains.

If they can do that, they can end their days in the knowledge that they have done what had to be done: "At the end of life you may close your eyes, stating: 'I have not been dominated by the Dominant Idea of my Age; I have chosen mine own allegiance and served it".[73]

* * *

Like many others, I have spent the whole of my adult life trying to understand what has gone wrong with our world and how we might identify and reach the path to a better future.

This is no easy task, given the numbers of lies, deceptions and traps deployed by the ruling caste so as to obstruct true understanding of the slave-system they have constructed and prevent any serious challenge to it.

But, like our sense of ethics, the Withway exists deep in our minds as an archetype of how we are meant to live.

Therefore, even when we cannot yet formulate it ourselves, we can usually recognise it when it is reflected in the ideas of other individuals or movements of thought.

The problem is that these reflections are fragments and the fact that one aspect of withness can be found in any source is no guarantee that it points us to the Withway as a whole.

Often we are encouraged by a promising sign to follow a particular path only to find that it quickly peters out in a tangle of incoherence.

Worst of all is the road that gradually veers from its promised course, without us even noticing, until it has performed a complete U-turn and we suddenly find ourselves marching, banners and placards still held proudly aloft, in exactly the opposite direction to that promised by our original intuition!

When we are young we imagine that a question as important as how we should best live must have already been resolved by the great minds of previous generations and that it is simply a question of finding one's way to the right philosophy, religion or ideology.

But as we get older, we realize that things aren't so simple and that in taking the beaten track of other people's thinking we usually find ourselves being led astray.

It is much better to stay awake and alert, to notice the hints and signs left by others but ultimately to rely on our own inner moral compass to guide us – our own sense of right and wrong and our own instinctive reactions to the ever-changing conditions of the society in which we are living.

"We must be governed by the guide within

rather than by the opinions of men",[74] as Aurobindo writes.

Because withness is within each of us, when we follow our own way we also follow the Withway.

* * *

We are finding our way back, all sorts of us from all over the place, straying back together, staying together some of us for a while to dig up the concrete and find the stars beneath.

Jenny James[75]

* * *

Our holistic awareness of withness allows us to see the world from a new and clear perspective and new layers of understanding come into view.

We see not only that we belong to humanity, to nature, to the cosmos, and that we are inseparable from the context in which we are situated, but we also realise how this withness has become invisible to modern people.

We therefore grasp that there is something important at stake with this idea of withness, that it is not just an abstract idea only of interest to navel-gazing day-dreamers, but has a very real impact on our world and our lives.

It is the lack of general awareness of with-ness which enables power to divide, control and exploit us, which allows us to accept its lies that nature is a raw resource and that destruction means progress. We are thus trapped in the sterile mindset of materialist modernity.

As our awareness grows, it becomes obvious to us that the Withway has not so much disappeared from view as been *hidden* from view, in the interests of power.

At this point, the Withway takes on a meaning that it would not have possessed in a different kind of society.

If all was largely well with our world, the Withway would amount to a simple continuation of the direction we were already taking, the maintenance of "an orderly society in harmony with nature"[76] urged by traditional Confucian philosophy in China.

But since this is far from being the case, it necessarily implies a radical breach with the status quo, so that we may rejoin the true path.

People who instinctively seek community, cohesion and continuity – a society founded on the natural order of withness – therefore find themselves confronted with the need to become revolutionaries.

Augustin Berque makes this point regarding Watsuji's insistence on *fûdosei*, on the importance of our symbiotic relationship with the places where we live, the grounding of our existences in a context of physical reality.

While today's rampant globalization systematically separates people from any sense of belonging to a particular place, "Watsuji's *mésologie* demonstrates that it is our very humanity that is at stake", he says. "For sure, in his day Watsuji was no revolutionary, but in the 21st century an idea like that carries the seed of a completely different world".[77]

Seeking the Withway necessarily implies rejecting the current system which has dragged us so far from it and urging others to do likewise.

Withness becomes a call to arms, a flag behind which free humanity can gather and prepare to engage.

As withness becomes visible as a cause, it inevitably comes under attack from power, at the very least on the level of smears and propaganda.

The idea of withness, sourced ultimately from the purest metaphysical level, thus climbs right down to the muddy battlefield of contemporary politics.

It turns into something else. It is no longer withness as reality, or withness as awareness of reality, but withness as a struggle to reassert itself as the guiding wisdom underlying human existence.

There is only one means by which it can become real and pro-active in the physical world, by which it can actually struggle: us.

If we make ourselves available as channels for the highest form of cosmic withness, we also make ourselves available as instruments for the restoration of withness on every level.

Our new holistic awareness shows us that the practical battles in which we are engaged on a human level are a down-reaching of higher principle.

Furthermore, when we have risen to the heights of metaphysical individuation, we descend to the practical realm of struggle *infinitely empowered* by this awareness.

Understanding that we are only transient physical manifestations of the universal light, we know that individual death has no meaning – our eternal essence is in the whole.

"No one is easier to terrorize than the person who believes that everything is over when his fleeting phenomenon is extinguished. The new slaveholders have realized this, and this explains the importance for them of materialistic theories",[78] writes Jünger.

"To overcome the fear of death is at once to overcome every other terror, for they all have meaning only in relation to this fundamental problem".[79]

The Withway is not just the knowledge of where we must go but the courage we need to take us there.

* * *

The moment of the rose and the moment of the
yew tree
Are of equal duration. A people without history
Is not redeemed from time, for history is a pattern
Of timeless moments

T.S. Eliot[80]

* * *

It has been the norm during my lifetime for
people to pretend that their individual lives take
place in a kind of bubble separated from the big
wide world outside.

All that really matters is your own little
story: your family, your relationships, your job,
your home, your tastes, your possessions, your
bank account, your pension scheme.

Having an opinion on the state of society as a
whole is an optional luxury. Taking that opinion
seriously enough to want to share it with lots of
other people is seen as eccentric; acting on it and
prioritising it over your own personal life is
regarded as alarmingly irresponsible.

It is, according to contemporary wisdom, not
only insane to focus on the bigger picture beyond
oneself but also futile, as mere individuals have

no possibility of influencing anything outside of their own domestic sphere.

In this way our society turns its back on one of the most important aspects of our overall withlife.

Watsuji's *fûdosei* not only embraces our belonging to others, and to the space we share with others, but also our belonging to time, our presence in a certain moment in history.

"The milieu is inseparable from history," he writes. "The movement of human self-understanding – the human in his characteristic duality of individual and social being – is at the same time historic. Consequently, there can no more be milieu separated from history than there can be history separated from milieu".[81]

His holistic overview insists that all history is rooted in place and all place is inseparable from history. If we try to understand them separately, we will be dealing only with abstract concepts, cut off from context and thus from reality.

The reality we describe as "politics" or "foreign affairs" or "progress" or "war" or "crisis" is the ground on which we stand.

It is as much a part of our full being as is our symbiotic relationship with place and people.

And just as we shape the landscapes in which we live and we shape the social connections which sustain us, so do we shape the society in which we live and the way in which it evolves.

If we neglect this essential role, shirk the responsibility and hide away inside the cowardly illusion of a purely individual existence, then we continue to shape society, but in a negative way – pushing it still further from the Withway.

Withness is present in time, as well as in place and people. It is the crest of an ever-breaking wave of history, as humans create ourselves, our milieux, our cultures, our traditions and our destinies in symbiosis with all that surrounds and sustains us.

Eliot writes that the historical sense involves a perception not only of the pastness of the past, but of its presence: "This historical sense, which is a sense of the timeless as well as of the temporal and of the timeless and the temporal together, is what makes a writer traditional. And it is at the same time what makes a writer most acutely conscious of his place in time, of his own contemporaneity".[82]

* * *

An epidemic of fear and despair has been sweeping the world since 2020, with liberties abolished, livelihoods lost, childhoods ruined, families divided, communities splintered, hearts broken, dreams shattered and lives left in ruins.

And yet, the seed of renewal can be found inside the darkest decay. This horrific sequence of events has also brought with it, despite itself, a glimmer of hope that it represents the beginning of the end of this malevolent historical era.

While millions have been taken in and swept away by the lies of power, millions of others have finally awoken.

In their arrogance, the ruling mafia have not even bothered to make sure their narratives are watertight, that their figures make sense and that their actions are coherent.

They have perhaps judged that their full-spectrum domination of global society has reached a point where they can get away with anything they want, without even making too much of an effort.

But they perhaps did not appreciate the full consequences of removing the long-worn velvet glove of "democracy" and exposing to public view the clenched fist of their venal greed, hypocrisy and violence.

People have not merely been able to see the real motivations, the real machineries, behind their so-called Great Reset, but are beginning to understand previous historical events in a different light.

In their now-notorious 2020 book boasting about their project, Klaus Schwab and Thierry Malleret of the World Economic Forum themselves provide a context for the shock-and-awe impact of the Covid spectacle.

They compare it with the 2001 atrocity in New York and gloat about the way that, after 9/11, "new security measures like employing widespread cameras, requiring electronic ID cards and logging employees or visitors in and out became the norm".[83]

If these spokesmen for tyranny can make the link, then suddenly it becomes considerably less "crazy" for opponents of their system to do the same thing.

Once someone has realised, through their own observation and research, that the world's international institutions, governments and media outlets have been systematically terrorising us with co-ordinated lies for their own nefarious purposes, that the "dodgy dossier" used to justify the invasion of Iraq in 2003 was merely usual practice on their part, then the door is open for all sorts of discoveries.

The idea that NATO, via its Gladio network, could have carried out false flag terrorist attacks across Europe in the second half of the twentieth century does not seem as outlandish as it may once have done.[84]

And, going back further, what about the Second World War? Schwab and Malleret cite it in the same breath as 9/11, describing it as "a transformative crisis of previously unimaginable proportions".[85]

The "fundamental changes to the global order and the global economy" it brought about included, of course, the post-war "Build Back Better" of US economic and cultural occupation of Western Europe.

When you combine this insight with an understanding of the financial networks which funded the Fascist and Nazi regimes, and thus helped bring about the war,[86] the official version of our recent history has begun to seriously unravel.

A political space has opened up since March 2020 in which it is possible to voice and share the kind of fundamental critique of the global system which was previously considered extremely marginal.

What I have been trying to convey in this book is that the nightmare imposed upon us under the New Normal is the logical conclusion of our departure from the natural order of the Withway and the domination of power, greed, money and industrial Technik.

If we succeed in resisting their new global dictatorship, and securing our freedom to decide our future, there will be no point in leaving intact all the infrastructures of oppression, all the weapons of control, which have brought us to this sorry point.

Do we want them to be taken up and used against us again by a slightly different gang of rulers, or by the same old gang in one of their regular new disguises?

* * *

For last year's words belong to last year's language
And next year's words await another voice

T.S. Eliot[87]

* * *

Millions are today awakening not just to the reality of the system, but to their own historical withness, the need to become an authentic individual by going beyond individualism, the need to find freedom by embracing responsibility.

It is easy to pretend that the vile reality of the death-cult system is nothing to do with us personally when its effects are suffered by *other* people, outside of our personal cocoon.

Why would we feel the need to *do* anything about bombs dropping on people's homes thousands of miles away, about *other people's* children in *other people's* countries being forced into slave labour or prostitution, about communities we know nothing about being torn from land we have never seen?

After all, we have our own livelihoods to

148

think about, our own families to care for, our own personal well-being to assure.

But today the system has turned its weapons on those who had until now been spared its worst excesses.

Suddenly, vast numbers of people find themselves unable to pretend that all is more or less well with the world.

Suddenly, they are discovering, in their hearts, the need to step forward and *participate* in the unfolding of our collective destiny, to *realise their historical withness.*

Once we have understood what is happening to us, once we have allowed that understanding to sink in, how can we not feel *obliged* to act?

"To know and not to do is as if our eyes saw the way but our feet refused to follow in it. In order of precedence, knowledge comes first, but in order of importance action, for while nothing can be done without knowledge, yet knowledge not acted upon is useless",[88] Kaibara Ekken advises us from 17th-century Japan.

Our ultimate destination need neither be imminent nor visible in order for us to be able to set off on the right path, he insists.

"Even a journey involving thousands of miles must begin with a single step. When going to a distant place, one must ever start from where one is".[89]

The Withway is an old way asking to become

the new way. It is the eternal way, the human way within the natural and universal way.

"What intense joy we can gain in sensing the wondrous phenomenon of Heaven and Earth – the light of the sun and the moon; the passing and re-passing of the four seasons; the changing shapes in cloud and mist; the mountain's profile; the dancing stream; the soft breeze; moisture of rain and dew; purity of snow; smile of flowers; growth of fragrant herbs; infinite life of birds, beasts, fishes and insects," writes Ekken.

"To make ourselves conversant with this wonderful nature is to expand our hearts, purify our feelings, arouse holy thoughts, and wash away all low and unclean desires. This is called inspiration, for the goodness which is within is aroused, and flows out at the touch of the outer world".[90]

When you have finished reading this, why not go outside and look up at the blue sky, the clouds or the stars?

Listen carefully. Even in the densest city, you will hear it. The call of an unseen bird. The giggle of an invisible child. Leaves set a-rustling by a breeze from beyond. Phantom faery voices singing of time long gone, of time yet to come.

Listen carefully. The Withway is calling us home.

ENDNOTES

Part I: Natural Withness

1. Augustin Berque, *Là, sur les bords de l'Yvette,* (Editions éoliennes, 2017), p. 46.
2. Augustin Berque, 'Milieu vivant, milieu humain, territoire et bien commun', 24èmes Rencontres d'été Abraham Mazel, 2-4 juillet 2021, Maison Mazel, Falguières, Saint-Jean-du-Gard, pp. 16-17.
3. Berque, *Là, sur les bords de l'Yvette*, p. 42.
4. Berque, *Là, sur les bords de l'Yvette*, p. 32.
5. Berque, *Là, sur les bords de l'Yvette*, p. 75.
6. Berque, *Là, sur les bords de l'Yvette*, p. 52.
7. Augustin Berque, Préface, *Watsuji Tetsurô, Fûdo: le milieu humain*, commentaire et traduction par Augustin Berque (Paris: CNRS Éditions, 2011), p. 27.
8. Berque, Préface, Watsuji, pp. 11-12.
9. Berque, *Là, sur les bords de l'Yvette*, p. 58.
10. Watsuji, p. 44.
11. Watsuji, p. 45.
12. T.S. Eliot, 'Tradition and the Individual Talent', *Selected Prose*, ed. by John Hayward (Middlesex: Penguin, 1953), p. 21.
13. Tu Wei-ming, 'Beyond the Enlightenment Mentality', Mary Evelyn Tucker and John A. Grim, eds, *Worldviews and Ecology: Religion, Philosophy,*

and the Environment (New York, Orbis Books, 1994), p. 27.

14. See Paul Cudenec, *The Stifled Soul of Humankind* (Sussex: Winter Oak, 2014).

15. Eliot, 'Tradition and the Individual Talent', *Selected Prose*, pp. 20-21.

16. Watsuji, p. 36.

17. Watsuji, p. 49.

18 .Watsuji, p. 212.

19. Peter Kropotkin, *Mutual Aid: A Factor of Evolution* (London: Freedom Press, 1993), p. 180.

20. Peter Kropotkin, *Ethics: Origin and Development* (Dorchester: Prism Press, n/d), p. 15.

21. Kropotkin, *Ethics*, p. 17.

22. Otto Gross, 'On the Phylogy of Ethics', 1902, *Selected Works 1901-1920*, trans. by Lois L. Madison (New York: Mindpiece, 2012), p. 15.

23. Otto Gross, 'Zur funktionellen Geistesbildung des Revolutionärs', *Werke 1901-20* (New York: Mindpiece, 2009), p. 355, cit. Gottfried M. Heuer, *Freud's 'Outstanding' Colleague/Jung's 'Twin Brother': The suppressed psychoanalytic and political significance of Otto Gross* (London & New York: Routledge, 2017), p. 101.

24. Edward Carpenter, *Civilisation: Its Cause and Cure, and other essays* (London: Allen & Unwin, 1921), p. 26.

25. Carpenter, p. 28.

26. Carpenter, p. 31.

27. *The Atharva Vida*, J .J. Clarke, ed., *Nature in Question: An Anthology of Ideas and Arguments* (London: Earthscan, 1993), p. 19.

28. John Cowper Powys, *The Meaning of Culture*

(London: Jonathan Cape, 1930), p. 73.

29. Powys, *The Meaning of Culture*, p. 72.

30. Powys, *The Meaning of Culture*, p. 130.

31. John Cowper Powys, *Autobiography* (London: Pan Books, 1982), p. 238.

32. Standing Bear, 'Land of the Spotted Eagle', *Nature in Question*, p. 26.

33. Crow-Apsaaloke *Ashkisshe* ceremony (sun dance). cit. John A Grim, 'Native North American Worldviews and Ecology', *Worldviews and Ecology*, p. 43.

34. Zhang Zai, 'The Western Inscription', cit. James D. Sellmann, 'Zhang Zai', *Great Thinkers of the Eastern World: The major thinkers and the philosophical and religious classics of China, India, Japan, Korea and the world of Islam*, ed. by Ian P. McGread (New York: HarperCollins, 1995), p. 110.

35. James D. Sellmann, 'The Spring and Autumn Annals of Master Lu', *Great Thinkers of the Eastern World*, p. 40.

36. Mary Evelyn Tucker, 'Ecological Themes in Taoism and Confucianism', *Worldviews and Ecology*, p. 157.

37. Kaibara Ekken, *The Way of Contentment*, trad. Ken Hoshino (Delhi: Facsimile Publisher, 2019), p. 30.

38. Mary Evelyn Tucker, 'Kaibara Ekken', *Great Thinkers of the Eastern World*, pp. 369-70.

39. Clarke, *Nature in Question*, p. 7.

40. Lao-Tzu, Tao Te Ching, *Nature in Question*, p. 23.

41. Maria Waser, *Begegnung am Abend: Ein Vermächtnis* (Stuttgart: Deutsche Verlags-Anstalt, 1933), p. 265, cit. Anne Harrington, *Reenchanted Science: Holism in German Culture from Wilhelm II to Hitler* (Princeton, NJ: Princeton University Press,

153

1999), p. 92.

42. Brian Branston, *The Lost Gods of England* (New York: Oxford University Press, 1974), pp. 52-53, cit. Gary R. Varner, *The Mythic Forest, the Green Man and the Spirit of Nature: The Re-Emergence of the Spirit of Nature from Ancient Times into Modern Society* (New York: Algora, 2006), p. 17.

43. Georges Lapierre, *Les ours prennent souvent la forme humaine* (pamphlet, 2016), p. 3.

44. Lapierre, p. 4.

45. Standing Bear, *Nature in Question*, p. 27.

46. Varner, p. 28.

47. Ralph Metzner, 'The Emerging Ecological Worldview', *Worldviews and Ecology*, p. 167.

48. James G. Cowan, *The Elements of the Aborigine Tradition* (Shaftesbury: Element Books Ltd, 1992), p. 2, cit. Varner, p. 15.

49. Friedrich Schelling, 'Ideas for a Philosophy of Nature', *Nature in Question*, p. 123.

50. Branston, cit. Varner, p. 17.

51. Robert Graves, *The White Goddess: A Historical Grammar of Poetic Myth*, ed. Grevel Lindop (Manchester: Faber & Faber, 1999), p. 413.

52. Varner, p. 28.

53. Paul Cudenec, *The Green One* (Sussex: Winter Oak, 2017), p. 25.

54. Watsuji, p. 102.

55. Watsuji, pp. 71-72.

56. Watsuji, p. 73.

57. Sir James George Frazer, *The Golden Bough: A Study in Magic and Religion*, ed. with an Introduction and Notes by Robert Fraser (Oxford: Oxford University Press, 2009), pp. 426-27.

58. Frazer, p. 409.

59. Frazer, p. 298.

60. Frazer, p. 551.

61. Frazer, p. 548.

62. Frazer, p. 538.

63. Frazer, p. 31.

64. Frazer, p. 525.

65. Frazer, p. 535.

66. Frazer, p. 534.

67. Frazer, p. 486.

68. Frazer, pp. 491-92.

69. Frazer, p. 487.

70. Graves, p. 375.

71. Graves, p. 357.

72. Frazer, p. 483.

73. Ibid.

74. Frazer, p. 399.

75. Frazer, p. 477.

76. Frazer, p. 455.

77. Frazer, p. 375.

78. Frazer, p. 494.

79. Frazer, p. 523.

80. Graves, p. 346.

81. Graves, p. 357.

82. Graves, p. 404.

83. Graves, p. 344.

84. Watsuji, p. 74.

85. Robert Fraser, Frazer, p. xx.

86. Fraser, Frazer, p. xxx.

87. Fraser, Frazer, p. xx.

88. Kropotkin, *Ethics*, pp. 50-51.

89. Kropotkin, *Ethics*, p. 53.

90. Kropotkin, *Ethics*, p. 16.

91. Kropotkin, *Ethics*, pp. 16-17.

92. Kropotkin, *Ethics*, p. 45.

93. Kropotkin, *Ethics*, p. 49.

94. Kropotkin, *Ethics*, p. 45.

95. Joseph S. Wu, 'Mencius', *Great Thinkers of the Eastern World*, p. 27.

96. Ibid.

97. Otto Gross, 'On the Symbolism of Destruction', *Selected Works*, p. 265.

98. Otto Gross, 'Protest and Morality in the Unconscious', *Selected Works*, p. 282.

99. William Wordsworth, 'Lines Written a Few Miles Above Tintern Abbey', *Nature in Question*, p. 128.

100. Berque, *Là, sur les bords de l'Yvette*, p. 87.

101. Watsuji, p. 274.

102. John Ruskin, cit. Stephen Coote, *William Morris: His Life and Work* (Oxford: Past Times, 1995), p. 21.

103. Alfred Noyes, *William Morris* (London: Macmillan & Co, 1908), p. 15.

104. John Ruskin, *Modern Painters I*, cit. *The Pre-Raphaelites* (London: Tate Gallery/Penguin, 1984), p. 12.

105. *The Pre-Raphaelites*, p. 11.

106. Ananda K. Coomaraswamy, *The Transformation of Nature in Art* (New York: Dover, 1956).

107. *What is Art? Conversation with Joseph Beuys*, ed. with essays by Volker Harlan, trans. by Matthew Barton and Shelley Sacks (West Hoathly: Clairview, 2014), p. 59.

108. *What is Art?*, p. 61.

109. *What is Art?*, p. 72.

110. *What is Art?*, p. 22.

111. Peter Ackroyd, *T.S. Eliot* (London: Penguin,

1988), p. 112.

112. Ackroyd, p. 70.

113. Ackroyd, pp. 269-70.

114. T.S. Eliot, 'The Music of Poetry', *Selected Prose*, p. 59.

115. See Paul Cudenec, *Nature, Essence and Anarchy* (Sussex: Winter Oak, 2016).

116. Herbert Read, cit. George Woodcock, *Herbert Read: The Stream and the Source* (Montreal/New York/London: Black Rose Books, 2008), p. 192.

117. Varner, p. 24.

118. Frazer, p. 12.

119. Joseph Campbell, *The Masks of God: Primitive Mythology* (London: Souvenir Press, 2011), p. 5.

120. Radmila Moacanin, *The Essence of Jung's Psychology and Tibetan Buddhism: Western and Eastern Paths to the Heart* (Boston: Wisdom Publications, 2003), p. 27.

121. Graves, p. 366.

122. C.G. Jung, *Psyche & Symbol: A Selection from the Writings of C.G. Jung*, ed. by Violet S. de Laszlo (New York: Anchor Books, 1958), pp. xv-xvi.

123. C.G. Jung, *The Archetypes of the Collective Unconscious* (Princeton: Princeton University Press, 1969), p. 48, cit. Moacanin, p. 31.

124. Moacanin, p. 31.

125. Moacanin, p. 76.

126. Silvia Federici, *Caliban and the Witch* (Brooklyn: Autonomedia, 2004), pp. 141-42.

127. Lapierre, p. 9.

128. Lapierre, p. 18.

129. Sarvepalli Radhakrishnan, *An Idealist View of Life* (London: Unwin Hyman, 1988), p. 43.

130. Sri Aurobindo, *The Synthesis of Yoga* (Pondicherrry, India: Sri Aurobindo Ashram Trust, 1973), p. 353.

131. Aurobindo, p. 354.

132. Chenyang Li, 'The Doctrine of the Mean', *Great Thinkers of the Eastern World*, p. 56.

133. Alan Fox, 'Fazang', Great Thinkers of the Eastern World, p. 101.

Part II: Lost in Falsehood

1. W.B. Yeats, 'The Stolen Child', *Selected Poetry* (London: Pan Books, 1974), p. 5.

2. Paul Cudenec, *The Anarchist Revelation: Being What We're Meant to Be* (Sussex: Winter Oak, 2013), p. 11.

3. Cudenec, *The Anarchist Revelation*, p. 1.

4. James C. Scott, *Against the Grain: A Deep History of the Earliest States* (New Haven and London: Yale University Press, 2017), p. 5.

5. Scott, p. 7.

6. Scott, p. 46.

7. Scott, pp. 25-27.

8. Scott, p. 241.

9. Scott, p. 245.

10. Scott, p. 152.

11. Scott, p. 180.

12. Hans J. Nissen and Peter Heine, *From Mesopotamia to Iraq: A Concise History*, trans Hans. J. Nissen (Chicago: University of Chicago Press, 2009), p. 31. cit. Scott, p. 161.

13. Scott, p. 29.

14. Scott, p. 146.

15. Scott, p. 151.

16. Scott, p. 146.

17. Scott, p. 144.

18. Guillermo Algaze, 'The End of Prehistory and the Uruk Period', *The Sumerian World*, ed. Harriet Crawford (London: Routledge, 2013), p. 81, cit. Scott, p. 160.

19. Scott, p. 169.

20. Scott, p. 167.

21. Peter Kropotkin, *Ethics: Origin and Development* (Dorchester: Prism Press, n/d), pp. 259-60.

22. Watsuji Tetsurô, *Fûdo: le milieu humain*, commentaire et traduction par Augustin Berque (Paris: CNRS Éditions, 2011), p. 148.

23. Scott, pp. 156-57.

24. Adam Hochschild, *Bury the Chains: Prophets and Rebels in the Fight to Free an Empire's Slaves* (New York: Houghton Mifflin, 2015), p. 2, cit. Scott, pp. 155-56.

25. Ester Boserup, *The Conditions of Agricultural Growth: The Economics of Agrarian Change Under Population Pressure* (Chicago: Aldine, 1965), p. 73, cit. Scott, p. 153.

26. T.S. Eliot, *The Rock*, *Selected Poems* (London: Faber & Faber, 1954), p. 121.

27. Ferdinand Tönnies, *Community and Society: Gemeinschaft und Gesellschaft*, trad. Charles P. Loomis, (New York: Dover Publications, 2002), p. 216.

28. Tönnies, p. 208.

29. Tönnies, p. 230.

30. Tönnies, p. 83.

31. Tönnies, p. 202.

32. Theodore Roszak, *The Cult of Information: A Neo-*

Luddite Treatise on High-Tech, Artificial Intelligence and the True Art of Thinking (Berkeley/Los Angeles/London: University of California Press, 1994), p. 159.

33. Roszak, pp. 159-60.

34. Organic Radicals, 'Anti-business and proud of it', www.orgrad.wordpress.com/articles

35. Silvia Federici, *Caliban and the Witch* (Brooklyn: Autonomedia, 2004), pp. 21-22.

36. Federici, p. 26.

37. Federici, p. 82.

38. Federici, p. 84.

39. Federici, p. 83.

40. Lawrence F. Hundersmarck, 'Mozi', *Great Thinkers of the Eastern World: The major thinkers and the philosophical and religious classics of China, India, Japan, Korea and the world of Islam*, ed. by Ian P. McGread (New York: HarperCollins, 1995), p. 16.

41. T.S. Eliot, 'Religion and Literature', *Selected Prose*, ed. by John Hayward (Middlesex: Penguin, 1953), p. 40.

42. Kropotkin, *Ethics*, p. 27.

43. Kropotkin, *Ethics*, p. 28.

44. John Cowper Powys, *The Meaning of Culture* (London: Jonathan Cape, 1930), pp. 309-10.

45. Otto Gross, 'On the Symbolism of Destruction', *Selected Works 1901-1920*, trans. by Lois L. Madison (New York: Mindpiece, 2012), p. 266.

46. Eliot, 'Yeats', *Selected Prose*, ed. by John Hayward (Middlesex: Penguin, 1953), p. 203.

47. Watsuji, p. 140.

48. Watsuji, pp. 146-47.

49. Roszak, p. 233.

50. Jacques Ellul, *Le bluff technologique* (Paris: Hachette, 2004), p. 502.

51. Ellul, *Le bluff technologique*, p. 38.

52. Ellul, *Le bluff technologique*, p. 36.

53. Roszak, p. 54.

54. Ellul, *Le bluff technologique*, p. 104.

55. Roszak, p. 62.

56. Ellul, *Le bluff technologique*, p. 90.

57. Roszak, p. 233.

58. Georges Bernanos, 'La France contre les robots', cit. *Aux origines de la décroissance – Cinquante penseurs*, coordonné par Cédric Biagini, David Murray, Pierre Thiesset (Paris: L'Échappée, 2017), p. 28.

59. Bernanos, cit. *Aux origines de la décroissance*, p. 31.

60. Jacques Allaire, *Aux origines de la décroissance*, p. 30.

61. Bernanos, cit. *Aux origines de la décroissance*, p. 31.

62. Paul Cudenec, *Nature, Essence and Anarchy* (Sussex: Winter Oak, 2016), p. 88.

63. Klaus Schwab with Nicholas Davis, *Shaping the Future of the Fourth Industrial Revolution: A Guide to Building a Better World* (Geneva: WEF, 2018), e-book, 27%.

64 Roszak, p. 143.

65. Roszak, p. 29.

66. Roszak, p. 204.

67. Roszak, p. 123.

68. Michael Bywater, *The Observer*, 1985, cit. Roszak, p. 123.

69. Roszak, p. 211.

70. Roszak, p. 164.

71. See wrenchinthegears.com.

72. See Paul Cudenec, *Fascism Rebranded: Exposing the Great Reset* (pdf, 2021), pp. 262-72.

73. Jean-Luc Porquet, Préface, Ellul, *Le bluff technologique*, p. 6.

74. Ellul, *Le bluff technologique*, p. 667.

75. Roszak, p. 44.

76. Ellul, *Le bluff technologique*, p. 74.

77. Porquet, Préface, Ellul, *Le bluff technologique*, p. 15.

78. Ellul, *Le bluff technologique*, p. 149.

79. Ellul, *Le bluff technologique*, p. 414.

80. Ellul, *Le bluff technologique*, p. 402.

81. Ellul, *Le bluff technologique*, pp. 396-97.

82. Ellul, *Le bluff technologique*, p. 296.

83. Ellul, *Le bluff technologique*, p. 51.

84. Ellul, *Le bluff technologique*, p. 181.

85. Ellul, *Le bluff technologique*, p. 689.

86. Roszak, p. 26.

87. Roszak, pp. 211-12.

88. Edgar Morin, *La Méthode*, vol 5, *L'humanité de l'humanité. L'identité humaine.* Seuil, 2001, pp. 221-22. cit. Guillaume Blanc, *L'invention du colonialisme vert: pour en finir avec le mythe de l'Eden africain* (Paris: Flammarion, 2020), p. 233.

89. Ellul, *Le bluff technologique*, p. 160.

90. Ellul, *Le bluff technologique*, p. 552.

91. Jacques Ellul, *Le système technicien* (Paris: Calmann-Lévy, 1977), p. 287, cit. *Serge Latouche présente Jacques Ellul, Contre le totalitarisme technique* (Neuvy-En-Champagne: Editions le passager clandestin, 2013), pp. 33-34.

92. Roszak, p. 241.

93. Eliot, *The Rock, Selected Poems*, p. 120.

94. Paul Cudenec, *The Anarchist Revelation: Being What We're Meant to Be* (Sussex: Winter Oak, 2013), p. 33.

95. Watsuji, p. 242.

96. Sarvepalli Radhakrishnan, *An Idealist View of Life* (London: Unwin Hyman, 1988), p. 223.

97. Ellul, Le bluff technologique, p. 393.

98. Roszak, p. 62

99. Roszak, p. xlvi.

100. Roszak, p. 75.

101. Ellul, *Le bluff technologique*, p. 107.

102. William Blake, 'Milton: A Poem', *Blake's Poems and Prophecies* (London: J.M. Dent & Sons, 1954), p. 110.

103. William Blake, *Complete Writings*, ed. by Geoffrey Keynes, (Oxford: Oxford University Press, 1972), p. 361, cit. Peter Marshall, *William Blake: Visionary Anarchist* (London: Freedom Press, 2008), p. 39.

104. Theodore Roszak, *The Voice of the Earth: An Exploration of Ecopsychology* (New York: Touchstone, 1993), p. 42.

105. Kathleen Raine, *William Blake* (London: Thames & Hudson, 1977), pp. 72-74.

106. Raine, p. 50.

107. Blake, 'Milton', Blake's Poems and Prophecies, p. 137.

108. *What is Art? Conversation with Joseph Beuys, ed. with essays by Volker Harlan*, trans. by Matthew Barton and Shelley Sacks (West Hoathly: Clairview, 2014), p. 23.

109. *What is Art?*, pp. 26-27.

110. *What is Art?* p. 57.

111. *What is Art?*, p. 89.

112. *What is Art?*, p. 22.

113. *What is Art?*, p. 21.

114. Guy Debord, *La société du spectacle* (Paris: Gallimard, 1992), p. 25.

115. Guy Debord, *Commentaires sur la société du spectacle* (Paris: Gallimard, 1992), p. 20.

116. Debord, *La société du spectacle*, p. 3.

117. Patrick Marcolini, *Le mouvement situationiste: une histoire intellectuelle* (Paris: L'Echappée, 2012), p. 202.

118. Miguel Amorós, 'Fondements élémentaires de la critique anti-industrielle', *Préliminaires: Une perspective anti-industrielle* (Villsavary: Éditions de la Roue, 2015), pp. 60-61.

119. Patrick Marcolini, 'Jaime Semprun', *Aux origines de la décroissance*, co-ordonné par Cédric Bagini, David Murray, Pierre Thiesset (Paris: L'Échappée, 2017), p. 279.

120. Marcolini, 'Jaime Semprun', *Aux origines de la décroissance*, p. 278.

121. William Morris, 'The Lesser Arts', *News From Nowhere and Selected Writings and Designs*, ed. by Asa Briggs (London: Penguin, 1984), p. 85.

122. Ellul, *Le bluff technologique*, p. 98.

123. Peter Ackroyd, *T.S. Eliot* (London: Penguin, 1988), p. 107.

124. Ackroyd, p. 242.

125. Ackroyd, p. 249.

126. T.S. Eliot, 'Conditions of Culture', *Selected Prose*, p. 248.

127. Ackroyd, p. 156.

128. Ackroyd, p. 24.

129. T.S. Eliot, 'Conformity to Nature', *Selected Prose*, p. 220.

130. Ackroyd, p. 88.

131. T.S. Eliot, 'The Responsibility of the Man of Letters in the Cultural Restoration of Europe, in *Norseman*, July/August 1944, cit. Ackroyd, p. 273.

132. T.S. Eliot, 'The Unity of European Culture', radio broadcast, 1946, cit. Ackroyd, p. 273.

133. Ackroyd, p. 273.

134. T.S. Eliot, 'The Reformation of Society', *Selected Prose*, p. 210.

135. Ellul, *Le bluff technologique*, p. 696.

136. Ellul, *Le bluff technologique*, p. 694.

137. Ellul, *Le bluff technologique*, p. 696.

138. Ellul, *Le bluff technologique*, p. 652.

139. Scott, p. 7.

140. Scott, p. 14.

141. Scott, p. 15.

142. Ibid.

143. Cudenec, *Fascism Rebranded*, p. 274.

144. Jacques Ellul, *L'illusion politique* (Paris: La Table Ronde, 2004), p. 218, cit. *Serge Latouche présente Jacques Ellul, Contre le totalitarisme technique*, p. 41.

145. T.S. Eliot, 'Christianity and Society', *Selected Prose*, p. 213.

146. Ellul, *Le bluff technologique*, p. 27.

147. Ellul, *Le bluff technologique*, p. 252.

148. Roszak, p. 23.

149. www.judibari.org/revolutionary-ecology.html

150. Jaime Semprun, René Riesel, *Catastrophisme,*

administration du désastre et soumission durable (Paris: Éditions de l'Encyclopédie, 2008), X.

151. Jaime Semprun, *Dialogues sur l'achèvement des temps modernes* (Paris: Éditions de l'Encyclopédie, 1993), p. 59.

152. Cory Morningstar, 'Act I, The Manufacturing of Greta Thunberg – for Consent: The Political Economy of the Non-Profit Industrial Complex', January 17, 2019, http://theartofannihilation.com/the-manufacturing-of-greta-thunberg-for-consent-the-political-economy-of-the-non-profit-industrial-complex/

153. Cory Morningstar, 'Act V, The Manufacturing of Greta Thunberg – for Consent: The Green New Deal is the Trojan Horse for the Financialization of Nature', February 13, 2019, http://theartofannihilation.com/the-manufacturing-of-greta-thunberg-for-consent-the-new-green-deal-is-the-trojan-horse-for-the-financialization-of-nature/

154. Ellul, *Le bluff technologique*, p. 425.

155. Cory Morningstar, 'The Great Reset: The final assault on the living planet', November 28, 2020, http://www.wrongkindofgreen.org/2020/11/28/the-great-reset-the-final-assault-on-the-living-planet-its-not-a-social-dilemma-its-the-calculated-destruction-of-the-social-part-iii/

156. Blanc, p. 210.

157. Blanc, pp. 29-30.

158. Cudenec, *Fascism Rebranded*, pp. 88-130.

159. Ackroyd, p. 157.

160. Ackroyd, p. 171.

161. T.S. Eliot, *Ash-Wednesday*, *Selected Poems*, p. 93.

162. Roszak, p. 103.

163. Radhakrishnan, p. 156.

164. Roszak, p. 18.

165. Roszak, pp. 231-32.

166. Roszak, p. 88.

167. Roszak, p. 71.

168. Roszak, p. 131.

169. Roszak, p. 127.

170. René Descartes, *Discours de la methode* (Paris: Flammarion, 2008), pp. 38-39, cit. Augustin Berque, *Là, sur les bords de l'Yvette: dialogues mésologiques* (Editions éoliennes, 2017), p. 41.

171. Berque, *Là, sur les bords de l'Yvette*, p. 41.

172. Berque, *Là, sur les bords de l'Yvette*, p. 85.

173. Berque, *Là, sur les bords de l'Yvette*, p. 40.

174. Renaud Garcia, *Le Sens des limites: contre l'abstraction capitaliste* (Paris: L'Échappée, 2018), p. 90.

175. Garcia, pp. 208-09.

176. Garcia, p. 210.

177. Carolyn Merchant, *The Death of Nature: Women, Ecology, and the Scientific Revolution* (San Francisco: HarperCollins, 1990), p. 68.

178. Ibid.

179. Georges Lapierre, *Les ours prennent souvent la forme humaine* (pamphlet, 2016), p. 11.

180. Radhakrishnan, p. 169.

181. Berque, *Là, sur les bords de l'Yvette*, p. 42.

182. William Anderson, *Green Man: The Archetype of our Oneness with the Earth* (London and San Francisco: HarperCollins, 1990), p. 154.

183. Robert Graves, *The White Goddess: A Historical Grammar of Poetic Myth*, ed. by Grevel Lindop (Manchester; Carcanet Press, Faber & Faber, 1999),

p. 472.

184. Graves, p. 449.

185. Roszak, p. 146.

186. Ackroyd, p. 182.

187. T.S. Eliot, *Thoughts After Lambeth* (London, 1931), cit. Ackroyd, p. 172.

188. Augustin Berque, 'Milieu vivant, milieu humain, territoire et bien commun', 24èmes Rencontres d'été Abraham Mazel, 2-4 juillet 2021, Maison Mazel, Falguières, Saint-Jean-du-Gard, p. 7.

Part III: Finding the Withway

1. Kaibara Ekken, *The Way of Contentment, trad. Ken Hoshino* (Delhi: Facsimile Publisher, 2019), p. 34.

2. Jacques Ellul, *Le bluff technologique* (Paris: Hachette, 2004), pp. 724-25.

3. James C. Scott, *Against the Grain: A Deep History of the Earliest States* (New Haven and London: Yale University Press, 2017), p. 139.

4. Scott, pp. 185-86.

5. Scott, p. 209.

6. Scott, p. 186.

7. Scott, p. 209.

8. Scott, p. 32.

9. Scott, p. 57.

10. Scott, p. 59.

11. Scott, p. 57.

12. Scott, p. 49.

13. T.S. Eliot, *Four Quartets* (London: Faber & Faber, 1955), p. 16.

14. Mohandas Gandhi, letter to Nehru, October 5, 1945, cit. Ranchor Prime, *Vedic Ecology: Practical*

Wisdom for Surviving the 21st Century (Novato, California: Mandala, 2002), p. 91.

15. Gandhi, 'Constructive Programme', cit. Prime, p. 87.

16. M.K. Gandhi, *The Village Reconstruction* (Bombay; Bharatiya Vidya Bhavan, 1966), p. 30, cit. Christopher Key Chapple, 'Hindu Environmentalism: Traditional and Contemporary Resources', Mary Evelyn Tucker and John A. Grim, eds, *Worldviews and Ecology: Religion, Philosophy and the Environment* (New York, Orbis Books, 1994), pp. 117-18.

17. Bharatan Kumarappa, *Capitalism, Socialism or Villagism* (Madras: Shakti Press, 1946), p. 58.

18. Kumarappa, p. 105.

19. Kumarappa, p. 192.

20. Watsuji Tetsurô, *Fûdo: le milieu humain*, commentaire et traduction par Augustin Berque (Paris: CNRS Éditions, 2011), p. 70.

21. Theodore Roszak, *The Cult of Information: A Neo-Luddite Treatise on High-Tech, Artificial Intelligence and the True Art of Thinking* (Berkeley/Los Angeles/London: University of California Press, 1994), p. 146.

22. Martin Buber, 'Alte und neue Gemeinschaft', cit. Michael Löwy, 'Martin Buber's Socialism', *Martin Buber: His Intellectual and Scholarly Legacy*, ed. Sam Berrin Shonkoff (Leiden: Koninklijke Brill, 2018), p. 133.

23. Martin Buber, cit. Michael Lowy, *Rédemption et utopie: le judaïsme libertaire en Europe centrale* (Paris: Editions du Sandre, 2009), p. 74.

24. T.S. Eliot, 'A Christian Community', *Selected*

Prose, ed. by John Hayward (Middlesex: Penguin, 1953), p. 215.

25. Tu Wei-ming, 'Beyond the Enlightenment Mentality', *Worldviews and Ecology*, p. 27.

26. Robert Graves, *The White Goddess: A Historical Grammar of Poetic Myth*, ed. by Grevel Lindop (Manchester; Carcanet Press, Faber & Faber, 1999), pp. 472-73.

27. Jacques Ellul, 'Autopsie de la révolution', *Serge Latouche présente Jacques Ellul, Contre le totalitarisme technique* (Neuvy-En-Champagne: Editions le passager clandestin, 2013), p. 99.

28. Gandhi, *The Village Reconstruction*, cit. Chapple, *Worldviews and Ecology*, p. 118.

29. Lawrence F. Hundersmarck, 'Mozi', *Great Thinkers of the Eastern World: The major thinkers and the philosophical and religious classics of China, India, Japan, Korea and the world of Islam,* ed. by Ian P. McGread (New York: HarperCollins, 1995), p. 17.

30. Hundersmarck, 'Mozi', *Great Thinkers of the Eastern World*, p. 16.

31. Clément Pansaers, *L'Apologie de la paresse* (Paris: Editions Allia, 2005), p. 48.

32. Leo Tolstoy, *A Calendar of Wisdom: Wise Thoughts for Every Day*, trans. Peter Sekirin (London: Hodder and Stoughton, 1998), p. 70.

32. Tolstoy, p. 229.

34. Tolstoy, p. 155.

35. Sri Aurobindo, *The Synthesis of Yoga* (Pondicherrry, India: Sri Aurobindo Ashram Trust, 1973), p. 184.

36. Joseph Campbell, *The Masks of God: Occidental Mythology* (Harmondsworth: Penguin, 1985), p. 449.

37. Benjamin Hennot, 'L'Apologie de la paresse de

Clément Pansaers', *Dits*, 21, Printemps 2016, p. 134.

38. Hennot, *Dits*, p. 137.

39. Hennot, *Dits*, p. 135.

40. Watsuji, p. 262.

41. Jacques Ellul, *Le bluff technologique* (Paris: Hachette, 2004), p. 439.

42. Ernst Jünger, *The Forest Passage*, trans. Thomas Friese, ed. Russell A. Berman (Candor, New York: Telos Press Publishing, 2013), p. 60.

43. Jünger, p. 29.

44. Aurobindo, p. 404.

45. Aurobindo, p. 203.

46. Aurobindo, p. 398.

47. Aurobindo, p. 52.

48. Aurobindo, p. 56.

49. Aurobindo, p. 43.

50. Aurobindo, pp. 464-65.

51. Alan Fox, 'Fazang', *Great Thinkers of the Eastern World*, p. 100.

52. James D. Sellmann, 'Cheng Hao and Cheng Yi', *Great Thinkers of the Eastern World*, p. 113.

53. Cheng Hao and Cheng Yi, *Great Learning*, cit. Sellmann, 'Cheng Hao and Cheng Yi', *Great Thinkers of the Eastern World*, p. 114.

54. Jacques d'Hondt, *Hegel et l'hégélianisme* (Paris: Que sais-je, Presses Universitaires de France, 1991), p. 56.

55. Frederick Beiser, *Hegel* (Abingdon: Routledge, 2005), p. 81.

56. Aurobindo, p. 185.

57. Aurobindo, p. 162.

58. Aurobindo, p. 50.

59. Aurobindo, p. 162.

60. John Cowper Powys, *The Meaning of Culture* (London: Jonathan Cape, 1930), p. 149.

61. Powys, *The Meaning of Culture*, p. 150.

62. Powys, *The Meaning of Culture*, p. 18.

63. Powys, *The Meaning of Culture*, p. 20.

64. Powys, *The Meaning of Culture*, p. 22.

65. Powys, *The Meaning of Culture*, p. 19.

66. Sarvepalli Radhakrishnan, *An Idealist View of Life* (London: Unwin Hyman, 1988), p. 162.

67. Radhakrishnan, p. 91.

68. Ibid.

69. C.G. Jung, *The Practice of Psychotherapy* (Princeton: Princeton University Press, 1966), p. 108, cit. Radmila Moacanin, *The Essence of Jung's Psychology and Tibetan Buddhism: Western and Eastern Paths to the Heart* (Boston: Wisdom Publications, 2003), p. 48.

70. Moacanin, p. 43.

71. Moacanin, p. 112.

72. Voltairine de Cleyre, 'The Economic Tendency of Freethought', *The Voltairine de Cleyre Reader*, ed. by A.J. Brigati (Oakland/Edinburgh, AK Press, 2004), p. 63.

73. Voltairine De Cleyre, 'The Dominant Idea', *The Voltairine de Cleyre Reader*, p. 45.

74. Aurobindo, p. 316.

75. Jenny James, *Atlantis alive: Love Letters from a Primal Commune* (Firle, Sussex: Caliban, 1980), p. 19.

76. Mary Evelyn Tucker, 'Ecological Themes in Taoism and Confucianism', *Worldviews and Ecology*, p. 152.

77. Augustin Berque, Préface, Watsuji, p. 29.

78. Jünger, p. 93.

79. Jünger, p. 51.

80. Eliot, *Four Quartets*, p. 43.

81. Watsuji, pp. 47-48.

82. T.S. Eliot, 'Tradition and the Individual Talent', *Selected Prose*, p. 23.

83. Klaus Schwab, Thierry Malleret, *Covid-19: The Great Reset* (Geneva: WEF, 2020), e-book. Edition 1.0. 60%

84. See Paul Cudenec, 'The Politics of Fear: Terrorism and State Control', *Antibodies, anarchangels and other essays* (Sussex: Winter Oak, 2013), pp. 73-98.

85. Schwab, Malleret, *Covid-19: The Great Reset*. 5%

86. See Paul Cudenec, *Fascism Rebranded: Exposing the Great Reset* (pdf, 2021).

87. Eliot, *Four Quartets*, p. 39.

88. Ekken, p. 77.

89. Ekken, p. 82.

90. Ekken, p. 31.

Also by Paul Cudenec

Full details of all these titles are available on the Winter Oak website at www.winteroak.org.uk, along with the regular information bulletin *The Acorn*. To get in touch with Winter Oak please email winteroak@greenmail.net or follow @winteroakpress on Twitter.

CPSIA information can be obtained
at www.ICGtesting.com
Printed in the USA
LVHW111056191222
735527LV00015B/195

9 782957 576821